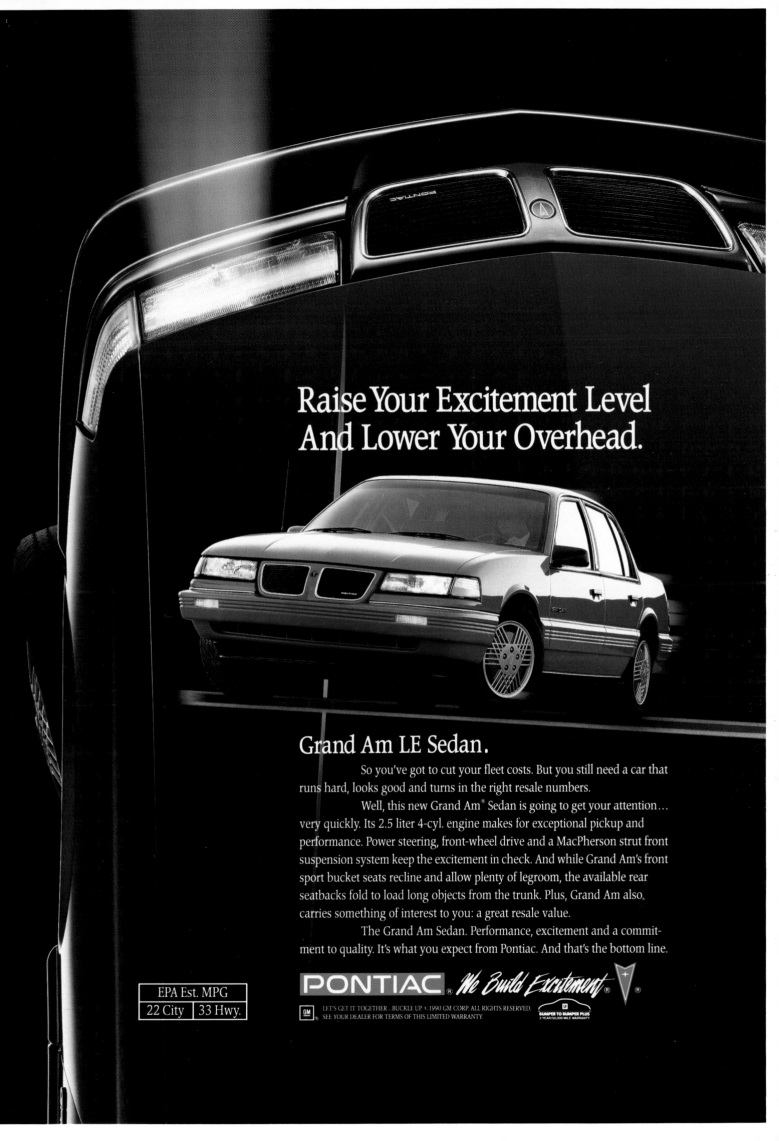

Raise Your Excitement Level And Lower Your Overhead.

Grand Am LE Sedan.

So you've got to cut your fleet costs. But you still need a car that runs hard, looks good and turns in the right resale numbers.

Well, this new Grand Am® Sedan is going to get your attention... very quickly. Its 2.5 liter 4-cyl. engine makes for exceptional pickup and performance. Power steering, front-wheel drive and a MacPherson strut front suspension system keep the excitement in check. And while Grand Am's front sport bucket seats recline and allow plenty of legroom, the available rear seatbacks fold to load long objects from the trunk. Plus, Grand Am also. carries something of interest to you: a great resale value.

The Grand Am Sedan. Performance, excitement and a commitment to quality. It's what you expect from Pontiac. And that's the bottom line.

EPA Est. MPG	
22 City	33 Hwy.

PONTIAC ® *We Build Excitement* ®

WINNER 1991 DAYTONA 500.

4OO HORSEPOWER

NEW KODAK GOLD 4OO NOW TRUST YOUR MEMORIES TO THE RICHEST, MOST SATURATED COLOR IN A HIGH-SPEED FILM. IT WILL STOP THE DAYTONA 500 IN ITS TRACKS. **SHOW YOUR TRUE COLORS.**™

WHEN IT COMES TO LIVE AUTO RACING, TNN IS IN THE DRIVER'S SEAT.

GET YOUR HEART RACING ON THE WEEKEND.

TNN: The Nashville Network offers over 20 **live** motorsports events. We are covering the biggest races **live**, including the Winston Cup Series, the Busch Grand National Series and the AC Delco Challenge Series.

And, with programs like *NHRA Today*, *TNN Motorsports Magazine*, and *Inside Winston Cup Racing*, we keep racing fans abreast of the latest race results and in touch with top drivers.

When it comes to America's fastest-growing sports nobody gets your motor running like TNN: The Nashville Network.

THE NASHVILLE NETWORK®

The Heart of Country

CONTENTS

Published By: Autosport International, Inc.
Publisher: John Norwood
Associate Publisher: Barbara H. Steig
Art Director: Robert Steig
Editor: Jonathan Hughes
Cover Art: LeRoy Neiman

Photographic Team: Dan Bianchi, Michael C. Brown, Linda McQueeney, Ron McQueeney, Dorsey Patrick, Steve Swope, and the photographic staff of Daytona International Speedway, headed by Bob Constanzo.

Daytona 500 by STP, The Men and Machines of Speed Weeks '91
is published by Autosport International, Inc., 79 Madison Avenue,
New York, NY, 10016
© 1991 by Autosport International, Inc.
No part may be reproduced without prior written permission.
Distributed in the U.S. by Motorbooks International, Osceola, WI, 54020
Printed in the U.S.A.

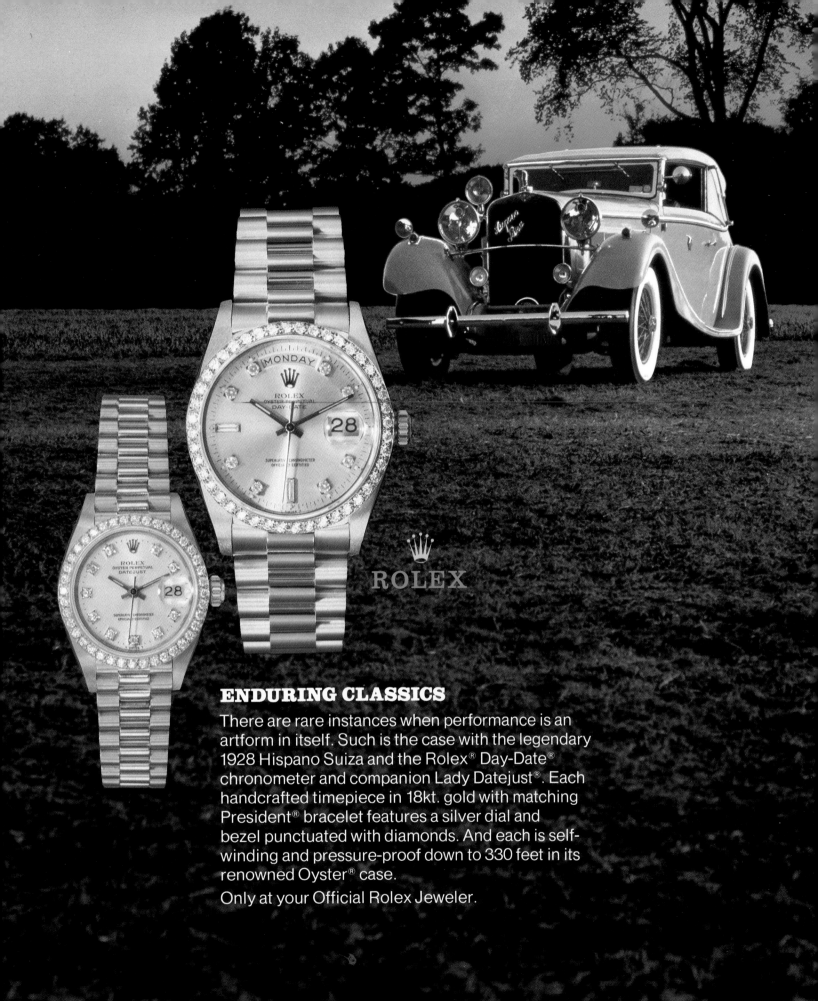

ENDURING CLASSICS

There are rare instances when performance is an artform in itself. Such is the case with the legendary 1928 Hispano Suiza and the Rolex® Day-Date® chronometer and companion Lady Datejust®. Each handcrafted timepiece in 18kt. gold with matching President® bracelet features a silver dial and bezel punctuated with diamonds. And each is self-winding and pressure-proof down to 330 feet in its renowned Oyster® case.

Only at your Official Rolex Jeweler.

Write for brochure. Rolex Watch U.S.A., Inc., Rolex Building, 665 Fifth Avenue, New York, NY 10022

NISSANS DENIED

Sporting a formidable array of high tech machinery and a highly capable driver cadre, the potent Nissan team was denied its goal of an overall victory. The driving team of Geoff Brabham, Chip Robinson, Derek Daly, and Bob Earl did salvage second place.

SUNBANK 24 AT DAYTONA FOR THE ROLEX CUP

FOR PORSCHE, A TIMELY RETURN TO THE WINNER'S CIRCLE
FOR HURLEY HAYWOOD, A RECORD FIFTH TITLE

With a little help from his friends, Franco/German teammates in a Joest entered, water-cooled Porsche 962C, Hurley Haywood became the first driver to post five Daytona endurance wins. Frenchman Bob Wollek, added to the original Haywood team of Frank Jelinski, "John Winter" (nom de course for a talented German driver and LeMans winner), and Henri Pescarolo, when his own polesitting Joest Porsche 962C exited the contest while in the lead, became a four-time winner.

As is often the case in endurance contests, the winners, who posted 719 laps, were not among the early leaders, regularly racking up lap speeds consistent with their 7th place qualifying slot. Eventual second place finishers (18 laps in arrears), Geoff Brabham, Chip Robinson, Derek Daly, and Bob Earl in the Nissan Performance Technology R90CK were the early pacesetters, along with the Bud Lite Jaguar XJ12 of Davy Jones, Derek Warwick, Raul Boesel, and Scott Pruett, followed by the second Nissan Group C LeMans-type car driven by Steve Millen, Bob Earl, and Jeremy Dale. The sole Jaguar to start fell early to engine failure at 379 laps. A second Jaguar crashed in qualifying. The second Nissan lasted 472 circuits. The Group C cars were invitational entries, denied the front row starting positions, and required to abide by FISA's more restrictive World Sportscar Championship rules for fuel allocation and fuel flow. In essence, the Group C cars, while faster on the track, were slower in the pits, A third Nissan R90CK, with Arie Luyendyk and Julian Bailey sharing

driving duties, was entered for "insurance" and withdrawn early. An "all Andretti" Porsche 962 for Mario, Michael, and Jeff ran with the leaders until it was forced off course by another competitor's rain-abetted spin. A new nose piece and some suspension parts returned it to the fray and a spot on the leader board until electrical problems slowed its second challenge. In the closing stages, Mario suffered the indignity of being passed by Robbie Gordon's Whistler Ford Mustang, the GTO leader, but still managed a fifth place finish. Gordon and teammates Mark Martin and Wally Dallenbach were spectacular in capturing GTO honors and fourth overall, somewhat ahead of teammates Dorsey Schroeder, Max Jones, and John Fergus who ended up sixth overall and second in GTO. Third overall went to the three year old Wynn's Porsche 962 in the hands of John Hotchkiss, James Adams, and Chris Cord, with an assist from Rob Dyson whose own 962 fell to mechanical problems. Seventh through ninth places went to Camel Lights cars; the Parker Johnstone, Doug Peterson, Steve Cameron, and Bob Lesnett Acura/B.F. Goodrich Spice was the category winner, followed by the Frank Jellinek Jr., John Grooms, Michael Greenfield, and Peter Greenfield Erie Scientific Mazda Kudzu and the Mike Dow, Andrew Hepworth Hendrick Ten Cate HDF Buick Spice. The top ten was rounded out by the Jim Stevens, Jim Jaeger, Craig Bennett, and Tom Grunnah Reliance Elevator Mustang. Mazda again prevailed in GTU via the Dick Greer, Mike

Mees, Peter Uria, and Al Bacon RX7. Thirteen was their lucky overall placement. Proceedings were enlivened by a late Saturday afternoon deluge which produced monster rooster tails and a couple of spins on the front straight.

While the rain lasted, Britisher James Weaver distinguished himself with quick, impeccable laps in the Dyson Porsche 962C co-driven by John Paul Jr., Tiff Needell, and owner Rob Dyson. Electrical problems and, later, an oil pump failure caused the engine to expire, and along with it, their chances of victory.

While no new overall records of note were set, except for Haywood's fifth victory, the race was again rated four stars for the variety and caliber of drivers entered. Roush Racing did set a new standard in GTO, seven straight victories, all with Ford Motor Co. products. In addition to stellar performers previously mentioned, the competitors included Indy Car champion Al Unser Jr., his father Al, clansmen Robby and Bobby in a new 962C that never got itself fully sorted, 1990 Daytona 500 winner Derrike Cope in the 11th place Milner Chevrolet Spice, Indy Car driver Rocky Moran, endurance star Derek Bell and son Justin in the fans' favorite entry, a "topless" Porsche 966, and dynamic Willy T. Ribbs, partnering Juan Fangio II in one of Dan Gurney's Toyota Eagles, which failed to go the distance.

NASCAR's Mark Martin, a standout on road circuits, competing in his fourth Daytona 24 Hour outing, called it a "safe race" from his view through the windshield of the GTO winning Whistler Ford Mustang.

MARTINI & ROSSI

TWO DECADES OF TOP SPORTING ACHIEVEMENTS CROWN A CENTURY OF QUALITY AND TRADITION

Synonymous with top sporting achievements for the past twenty years, the famous red and blue stripes of Martini Racing have today become a familiar sight for motorsport and powerboat racing enthusiasts the world over.

An exacting blend of elegance and performance, the team's approach to competition is a reflection of the qualities that have helped make Martini & Rossi the world's sixth most important wines and spirits group.

Martini & Rossi's roots go back to 1863 in Piedmont, Northern Italy, and their product knew a wide success with early exports to other continents. As far back as 1887, from the port of Genoa alone more than 300,000 cases were shipped to the United States, South America, Egypt and the Far East.

Taking off from there, Martini & Rossi has recorded continuous success thanks to excellent quality and faithfulness to tradition: an industrial development which also looks with interest to cultural and sporting events. Martini & Rossi's Museum of the History of Oenology at Pessione, in Piedmont, is visited by thousands of people every year.

Nowadays Martini & Rossi is the principal asset of the General Beverage Corporation, a privately held company with 4,000 employees manufacturing and selling over 300 products through 80 subsidiaries and affiliates all over the world.

With a sales volume of 400 million bottles a year, valued at more than $1 billion, the Martini

For Martini / Lancia, a fourth consecutive World Rally Championship.

& Rossi Group is ranked 6th worldwide among all wine and spirits producers. Martini is the second largest selling single brand worldwide.

Besides being world leader for wine based aperitifs, the Martini & Rossi Group holds an important share in the sparkling wines market particularly with Martini & Rossi Asti Spumante, as well as in port, with Offley Port. They are present in the spirits market, too, with their whiskeys, William Lawson's and Glen Deveron, with cognac, Gaston de Lagrange, and liqueur, Bénédictine.

The famous recipe of Martini & Rossi Vermouth starts from a dry white wine, produced after a strict selection of grapes, which year after year, is held to the same high quality standards.

An alcoholic infusion of herbs, leaves, flowers, seeds, and roots taken from 33 different plants gives Martini & Rossi its aroma and characteristic taste, makes

the secret of Martini which, since 1863, has been pleasing customers around the world.

Martini & Rossi Rosso, Bianco, Dry, Rosé, are four different flavors, each different, each pleasurable.

Straight, in cocktails, or as a long drink, Martini & Rossi's adaptability is unmatched.

For twenty years, this "art de vivre" and insistence on quality have had their parallel in the world of motorsports. In association with some of racing and rallying's elite, such as Brabham, Lancia, Porsche, and Lotus the famous red and blue stripes of Martini & Rossi have accompanied hundreds of victories in such prestigious events as the LeMans 24 Hours, the Monte Carlo Rally, the Safari and many others. Martini & Rossi teams' standards have made it a force to be respected, a rewarding tribute to the passion that is Martini Racing.

EIGHTEEN
LAPS AHEAD
A victory margin of 18 laps, 2 minutes, 2.469 seconds at the end of the 24 Hours gave Hurley Haywood, aided by a veteran team of endurance drivers, his fifth Daytona 24 Hours victory, a new record.

MUSTANGS SHOW THEIR HEELS TO GTO FIELD

Yielding only to three all out prototypes, two Porsches and a Nissan, Robby Gordon, with co-drivers Wally Dallenbach Jr. and NASCAR's Mark Martin, brought a Roush Ford Mustang home first in GTO, fourth overall. The Roush team nailed down the top three GTO places. Max Jones, Dorsey Schroeder, and John Fergus piloted the second Mustang, Jim Stevens, Jim Jaeger, Craig Bennett, and Tom Grunnah the third. It was a repeat performance for Roush and Ford Motor Company since Mercury Cougars took the top GTO honors in the '90 Daytona 24 Hours. Gordon had the pleasure of chasing down and passing Mario Andretti in a slightly "off-song" Porsche in the closing stages of the race.

13

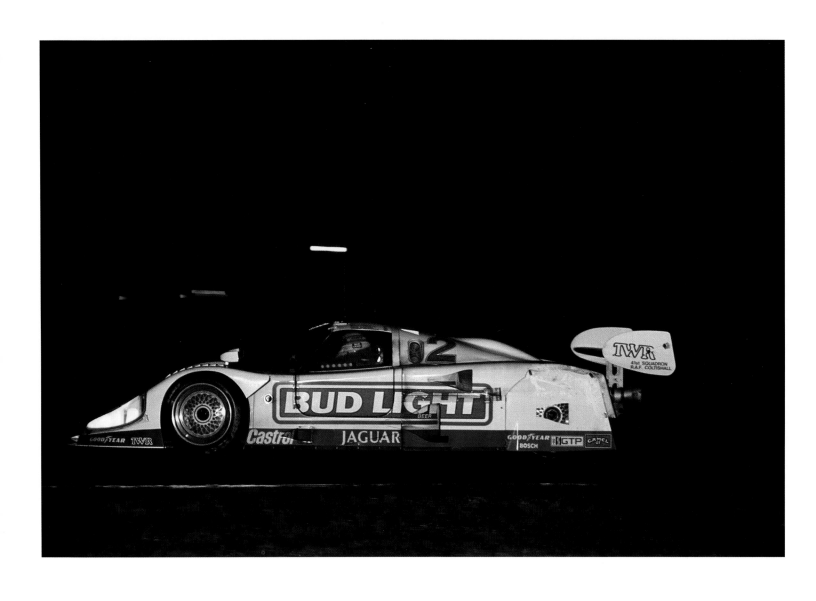

JAGUARS TOPPLED

All conquering in the '90 Daytona 24 Hours, the Walkinshaw Jaguars disappointed "cat" fans looking for a repeat victory. John Neilsen crashed one car in qualifying, too badly to run. The second in the hands of Davy Jones, Scott Pruett, Derek Warwick, and Raul Boesel managed only 30th place.

FIN POS	CLS POS	STR POS	CAR NO.	DRIVERS	ENTRANT	CAR	LAPS	STATUS
1	1	7	7	JOHN WINTER / FRANK JELINSKI / HENRI PESCAROLO / HURLEY HAYWOOD / BOB WOLLEK	Joest Porsche	Porsche 962	719	Running
2	1X	4	83X	GEOFF BRABHAM / CHIP ROBINSON / DEREK DALY / BOB EARL	Nissan Performance	Nissan R90C	701	Running
3	2	12	10	JOHN HOTCHKIS / JAMES ADAMS / CHRIS CORD / ROB DYSON	Wynns	Porsche 962	692	Running
4	1+	22	15+	ROBBY GORDON / MARK MARTIN / WALLY DALLENBACH, JR.	Whistler / Mustang	Ford Mustang	672	Running
5	3	6	00	MARIO ANDRETTI / MICHAEL ANDRETTI / JEFF ANDRETTI	Dauer Rcg	Porsche 962C	663 NR	Engine
6	2+	21	12+	DORSEY SCHROEDER / MAX JONES / JOHN FERGUS	Whistler / Mustang	Ford Mustang	658	Running
7	1L	16	48L	PARKER JOHNSTONE / DOUG PETERSON / STEVE CAMERON / BOB LESNETT	Acura / BF Goodrich	Acura Spice	654 NR	Electrical
8	2L	30	36L	FRANK JELLINEK, JR. / JOHN GROOMS / MICHAEL GREENFIELD / PETER GREENFIELD	Erie Scientific Rcg	Mazda Kudzu	632	Running
9	3L	28	54L	MIKE DOW / ANDREW HEPWORTH / HENDRIK TEN CATE	HDF Mtrsprts	Buick Spice	620 NR	Mechanical
10	3+	26	90+	JIM STEVENS / JIM JAEGER / CRAIG BENNETT / TOM GRUNNAH	Reliance Elevator	Ford Mustang	619	Running
11	4	14	4	BRIAN BONNER / JEFF KLINE / DERRIKE COPE / SCOTT SHARP	Tom Milner Rcg	Chevrolet Spice	611	Running
12	4+	24	92+	R. K. SMITH / JOE VARDE / DOC BUNDY / ANDY PILGRIM	Eds / Mobil / Goodyear	Chevrolet Corvette	611	Running
13	1*	36	82*	DICK GREER / AL BACON / PETER URIA / MIKE MEES	Greer Rcg	Mazda RX-7	605	Running
14	5+	17	63+	PRICE COBB / BRIAN REDMAN / JOHN O'STEEN / PETE HALSMER	Mazda	Mazda RX-7	576	Running
15	2*	35	37*	HONORATO ESPINOSA / ROB WILSON / FELIPE SOLANO / MIGUEL MOREJON	Botero Rcg Team	Mazda MX-6	576	Running
16	3*	31	38*	ROGER MANDEVILLE / KELLY MARSH / AMOS JOHNSON	Mandeville Auto Tech	Mazda RX-7	568	Running
17	4L	40	42L	GEOFF NICOL / TODD BRAYTON / DAVID TENNYSON	Intersport Rcg	Mazda Tiga	556	Running
18	5L	23	09L	TOMMY JOHNSON / ROB ROBERTSON / JOHN SHELDON / STEPHEN HYNES	R J Rcg	Buick Tiga	545	Running
19	4*	41	26*	ALEX JOB / CHRIS KRAFT / JACK REFENNING / JOE PEZZA	Border Cantina	Porsche 911	494	Running
20	2X	5	84X	JULIAN BAILEY / STEVE MILLEN / JEREMY DALE / ARIE LUYENDYK	Nissan Performance	Nissan R90C	472 NR	Mechanical
21	6+	25	91+	JOHN HEINRICY / DON KNOWLES / STUART HAYNER / SCOTT LAGASSE / TOMMY MORRISON	Eds Mobil Goodyear	Chevrolet Corvette	464	Running
22	5	10	16	JOHN PAUL, JR. / JAMES WEAVER / TIFF NEEDELL	Dyson Rcg	Porsche 962C	450 NR	Engine
23	5*	44	72*	JAY KJOLLER / PATRICK MOONEY / STEVE VOLK	Jay Kjoller Mtrsprts	Porsche 911	449	Running
24	6	15	5	MICHAEL BROCKMAN / JEFF DAVIS / TIM MCADAM / FRED PHILLIPS	Tom Milner Rcg	Chevrolet Spice	448 NR	Engine
25	7+	19	70+	MIKE NOLAN / ROGER SCHRAMM / PETER CUNNINGHAM / LOU GIGLIOTTI / BORIS SAID	M / J Engineering	Oldsmobile Cutlass	445	Running
26	6*	38	66*	BRAD HOYT / LEIGHTON REESE / MIKE GAGLIARDO	North Coast Rcg	Mazda RX-7	442 NR	Engine
27	8+	37	11+	JON GOODING / NORT NORTHAM / JOHN ANNIS / TOM PANAGGIO / MARK KENNEDY	Pepsi Cola	Chevrolet Camaro	427	Running
28	7	11	98	ROCKY MORAN / P. J. JONES / MARK DISMORE	All American Racers	Toyota Eagle	408 NR	Engine
29	9+	34	87+	ANTHONY PULEO / DANIEL URRUTIA / GRANT HILL / JACK BOXSTROM / NICK HOLMES	A&R Auto Electric	Chevrolet Camaro	396	Running
30	8	2	2	DAVY JONES / SCOTT PRUETT / DEREK WARWICK / RAUL BOESEL	Bud Light Jaguar Rcg	Jaguar XJR-12	379 NR	Engine
31	9	1	6	BOB WOLLEK / PAOLO BARILLA / BERND SCHNEIDER / MASSIMO SIGALA	Joest Porsche	Porsche 962C	360 NR	Engine
32	6L	20	9L	CHARLES MORGAN / JIM HESSERT / JIM PACE	Essex Rcg	Buick Kudzu	359 NR	Oil Leak
33	7L	32	20L	MICHAEL SHEEHAN / KAMING KO / CHARLIE MONK / RON MCKAY	Carlos Bobeda Rcg	Chevrolet Tiga	328 NR	Mechanical
34	10+	45	45+	BOB HUNDREDMARK / JOHN FORBES / KEN FENGLER / TOM CURRAN	First Coast Trucks	Chevrolet Corvette	315	Running
35	10	9	0	AL UNSER, SR / AL UNSER, JR / BOBBY UNSER / ROBBY UNSER	Dauer Rcg	Porsche 962C	270 NR	Accident
36	11+	46	28+	DON ARPIN / JON OLCH / TIM BANKS / SCOTT WATKINS	Drivers Alert Inc.	Chevrolet Camaro	234 NR	Engine
37	12+	27	53+	RICHARD MCDILL / BILL MCDILL / JIM BURT	TIC Financial Systems	Chevrolet Camaro	223 NR	Mechanical
38	7*	29	96*	BOB LEITZINGER / DAVID LORING / CHUCK KURTZ / DON REYNOLDS	Fastcolor Auto Art	Nissan 240SX	192 NR	Engine
39	8*	42	57*	REED KRYDER / ALISTAIR OAG / HENRY CAMFERDAM / PHIL KRUEGER	Kryderacing	Nissan 240SX	159 NR	Accident
40	11	13	60	DEREK BELL / JAY COCHRAN / JUSTIN BELL	BF Goodrich	Gunnar 966 Porsche	83	Running
41	13+	39	04+	BOB SCOLO / STEVE BURGNER / JOHN MACALUSO	Spirit of Brandon	Chevrolet Camaro	78	Running
42	12	8	99	JUAN FANGIO II / WILLY T RIBBS / ANDY WALLACE	All American Racers	Toyota Eagle	60 NR	Engine
43	14+	18	62+	CALVIN FISH / JOHN MORTON	Mazda	Mazda RX-7	50 NR	Accident
44	3X	3	1X	ARIE LUYENDYK / JULIAN BAILEY	Nissan Performance	Nissan R90C	47 NR	Mechanical
45	15+	43	06+	HOYT OVERBAGH / OMA KIMBROUGH	Overbagh Motor Rcg	Chevrolet Camaro	37 NR	Engine
46	9*	33	95*	BUTCH LEITZINGER	Fastcolor Auto Art	Nissan 24SX	13 NR	Mechnical

TIME OF RACE: 24:00:15.399   **L** = Camel Lights   **+** = GTO   ***** = GTU   **X** = LeMans Cars
WINNING SPEED: 106.633 mph for 719 laps (2,559.640 miles)   **NR** = Not running at finish
MARGIN OF VICTORY: 18 laps, 2 minutes, 2.469 seconds   **REC** = New record

FASTEST LAPS: GTP: Davy Jones, lap 24, 126.828 mph REC;
LeMans Cars: Julian Bailey, lap 518, 128.461 mph REC;
Camel Lights: Parker Johnstone, lap 334, 114.254 mph REC;
GTO: Wally Dallenbach, Jr., lap 421, 112.248 mph;
GTU: Roger Mandeville, lap 27, 103.590 mph

A TIMELY WIN FOR HURLEY HAYWOOD

Aided and abetted by a polished team of co-drivers, John Winter, Frank Jelinski, Henri Pescarolo, and Bob Wollek; Hurley Haywood netted his fifth Daytona 24 Hours victory. With it goes the Rolex Cup for the mantle and a Rolex watch for each of the drivers. Rolex Watch USA President, Roland Puton, makes the presentation with a smile.

PORSCHE REGAINS 24 HOURS TITLE

The winningest marque in Daytona 24 Hours history, Porsche regained its manufacturer's honors in '91. Rolex Watch's Roland Puton presented the newly rediscovered and totally refurbished Continental trophy to Porsche North America, headed by Brian Bowler.

GOODYEAR'S NATIONAL HIGHWAY HEROES HONORED AT DAYTONA

Highway Heroes Ken Bass, Jeff Lutz, Jim Williams, and Dale Beach with Goodyear's Tom Barrett.

Before the heroes of the high banks displayed their skill on the 2.5 mile trioval in the Daytona 500, some equally courageous drivers were honored at the Speedway. These drivers make their livings on the nation's highways, piloting the trucks that keep the country operating. In the course of crisscrossing the 49 states they occasionally run into situations where an instantaneous response can save a life. Driver Ken Bass of Milton, FL pushing his Western Star rig along a lonely Florida highway at night, saw a splash too big for an alligator. It had been produced by a car, plunging off a bridge into a river. He stopped, pulled the seatbelted but unconscious driver out of the overturned car, not without some difficulty. Driver James Williams of Leesville, LA pulled an elderly couple out of their burning car. Jeff Lutz of Albuquerque, NM had to break into a burning car to drag its two occupants to safety. Dale Beach of Wapwallopen, PA did the same for two teenage brothers. An impartial jury awarded Bass the "National Hero" title and runner-up honors to the other three.

Goodyear's Tom Barrett introduced the heroic truckers and made the awards; a $20,000 savings bond for Bass, $5,000 bonds for the remaining trio. Goodyear's Highway Hero Dept. 798, 1144 East Market Street, Akron, OH, 44316, will accept nominations for the 91/92 awards program covering the period of October 1, 1990 to September 30, 1991.

SPEED WEEKS 1991

SPEED WEEKS
AWARDS TOP BILLING TO THE FIRST EVER
DAYTONA 500 BY STP

How we look to the average

Over the years, STP® has been proud to be associated with some of the fastest names in NASCAR racing. The most famous is, of course, the legendary Richard Petty. 1991 marks our 20th anniversary with the "King." That's the longest driver sponsored relationship in motor sports history. And this year we're announcing the beginning

spectator at the Daytona 500.

of another relationship: entitlement sponsor of the 1991 Daytona 500 by STP. So look for our familiar oval wherever NASCAR races and do what so many people do. Use STP Oil Treatment and Newer Car Oil Treatment for extra engine protection. STP. The Edge.

DAYTONA 500 BY

In the emotion filled atmosphere generated by Desert Storm, rumbling thousands of miles to the East, but ever so close to home for many in the capacity crowd, First Brands Chairman and CEO Alfred E. Dudley welcomed more than 100,000 American flag waving racing enthusiasts to the 33rd Daytona 500, the first ever presented by STP. Honorary starter for the race, Dudley was introduced by the Speedway's new President, Jim Foster. Dudley expressed STP's pride in its selection as the first entitlement sponsor in the long and exciting history of the premier event in stock car racing. He went on to note that the association was a natural one, linking three racing entities synonymous with excellence, the Daytona 500, STP, and Richard Petty. The Petty legend is well known to racing fans; his seven Daytona 500 wins, flying the STP colors, a record unlikely to be broken, except perhaps by Richard himself. His third place qualifying position in the '91 edition of the classic indicates that the talent and the desire are still there.

"For the past 33 years, the toughest competitors in NASCAR have met in Daytona Beach to test their machines and stamina against each other and against the physical laws of nature. It has been a history filled with racing

excitement—from the first Daytona 500 in 1959, where Lee Petty was declared the victor after three days of photo-finish deliberations, to 1990's surprising win by Derrike Cope over Dale Earnhardt.

Supporting motorsports has been STP's commitment for more than three decades. Our commitment reaches back to 1959, when the STP logo first appeared on the specially built car "City of Salt Lake", driven by Athol Graham in an unofficial record attempt on the salt flats in Bonneville, Utah.

Thanks to Graham's raw courage, with the extra protection of STP Oil Treatment, the bullet-shaped City of Salt Lake recorded a top speed of 344.761 mph that day. Just like hundreds of racing competitors STP supported in later years, Graham found STP to be a positive driving force behind his success.

The history of STP is as legendary as the list of drivers who have helped make the three-letter logo synonymous with racing and winning—Mario Andretti and his sons Michael, Jeff and nephew John; Richard and Kyle Petty; Gordon Johncock; Bobby and Al Unser and Al Unser Jr.; Graham Hill, Parnelli Jones; Tom Sneva; Art Pollard; Jimmy Clark; Jim Hurtubise; Wally Dallenbach; Bobby Allison; Buddy Baker;

Paula Murphy and Don Prudhomme. Today, the STP heritage continues with Richard Petty in NASCAR, Bobby Rahal in CART/Indy Cars and Rickie Smith in NHRA drag racing action.

STP's involvement in stock car racing took shape in the early 70s, after the company had spent 14 years establishing a solid relationship with the Formula One and Indy Car fraternities. We strongly believed then that stock car racing would be a great new environment for STP products, and in the 1971 season signed Daytona 500 winner Fred Lorenzen as STP's first stock car driver.

The following season STP moved its sponsorship support behind the Petty Racing Team and driver Richard Petty. This gave birth to the most well known and successful driver-sponsor relationship in stock car history. With 200 career wins, seven Daytona 500 victories, and hundreds of other racing records to his credit, Richard Petty is truly The King of NASCAR racing. We are proud to celebrate his 20th anniversary with STP this season.

First Brands is committed to maintaining STP Racing's role as a major supporter of NASCAR Winston Cup stock car racing. STP's entitlement sponsorship of this year's Daytona 500 reflects the genuineness of our commitment."

A highly enthusiastic crowd unfurls a blanket of 100,000
American flags prior to the start of the Daytona 500 by STP.

NASCAR'S LONGEST...

STP'S RELATIONSHIP WITH RICHARD
PETTY COVERS 20 YEARS AND
200,000 RACING MILES

"I guess when you look at all the records and stuff,
there really is a lot we have accomplished with STP. But
we're not finished yet, there's still lots of time to add a
few more records to the list."

—Richard Petty

In an age where disposability is often accepted as the norm, STP's sponsor relationship with Richard Petty stands out as a model of durability, covering, as it does, 20 years and more than 200,000 racing miles, studded with seven Daytona 500 wins. In a ceremony prior to the '91 Daytona 500, Rick Bowen, Vice President, Marketing, First Brands, STP's parent company, presented the racing legend with a "token of gratitude" befitting a partnership of this magnitude. Obviously, no plaque, no painting, no piece of jewelry could match King Richard's accomplishments. Bowen came up with an eminently appropriate tribute, an outsize "check" for $1 million, symbolic of the $1 million principal amount annuity purchased by STP with Richard as the beneficiary. Payments are to start on the day of Richard's retirement as an active driver, a day only he can set. When he hangs up his helmet, Richard can watch the youngsters take aim at his records in the warm glow of financial security, a comforting condition that has eluded all too many star athletes, drivers included.

"Signing Petty prior to the 1972 season was a milestone in STP history," says Bowen. "It was the next logical step for STP, which had 12 previous years of experience in supporting Formula One and Indy Car racing. By extending its support into NASCAR Winston Cup with Petty and the Petty Racing Team, STP reinforced its commitment to make racing a partner with its products. And today, as a result of those efforts, most NASCAR teams use STP products."

During that first year with STP, Petty, with 13 years of NASCAR racing experience with the world famous Petty Racing Team under his helmet, won 21 Winston Cup races and captured his fourth NASCAR Championship. Soon after Petty joined STP, the King won back-to-back Daytona 500s, in 1973 and 74, the latter race shortened to 450 miles due to the energy shortage of the early 70s. The wins are an amazing record that still stands today as a tribute to Petty's determination and competitive ability.

As STP's man behind the wheel, Petty has set more records than any other NASCAR driver, including 200 career wins, more than 1100 starts (with 513 being consecutive starts), seven NASCAR Winston Cup championships, an unprecedented seven Daytona 500 wins, and nine Most Popular Driver awards. Highlighting Petty's list of accomplishments with STP is his being awarded NASCAR's Award of Excellence in 1987.

The most dramatic feat in Petty's career while carrying the STP banner may have occurred on the anniversary of our nation's birthday, July 4, 1984, when he scored his 200th career victory by winning the Pepsi 400 at Daytona International Speedway. The win was witnessed by a national television audience of millions and included a live visit from President Reagan, the only occasion on which a president has attended a NASCAR race. The race has gone down in STP history books as the most famous of all Pepsi 400 events, as Petty beat Cale Yarborough by inches.

When asked about his lengthy list of racing records, the always humble Petty once replied, "Well, to be honest, all the records that STP and the boys at Petty Enterprises have helped me win aren't the most important. I've said, as long as I can remember, that records never did mean a thing to me. What's mattered more…and still does…is what the next race is going to bring. You've always got to look ahead in this business, because once you start looking back at what you've accomplished, you're going to find yourself in trouble."

"Together, STP and Richard Petty are a great team, and I am looking forward to continuing the relationship as long as I am driving in NASCAR," Petty continued. "We've had good times and bad times in our days, but we've always managed to stick together and be successful."

Petty's distinctive lanky frame, down-to-earth personality and trademark cowboy hat and STP sunglasses have helped make him a legend in American racing folklore. Most racing experts agree that these qualities, and his contributions to driver safety both on and off the track, have enabled Petty to elevate stock car racing's popularity more than any other single factor or individual.

"No other NASCAR driver could be as an effective product spokesperson as Richard Petty," Rick Bowen commented. "Besides his contributions to racing, Petty helped make STP and its products household words. STP couldn't be happier with the relationship…it's been built on the same commitment to motorsports that gave STP its exciting start in the late 50s.

"That's why the 1991 NASCAR season means so much to STP," Bowen pointed out. "Not only is Richard Petty celebrating his 20th anniversary with STP this season, but STP has become the Daytona 500's first entitlement sponsor, an unprecedented move in the history of NASCAR event sponsorship."

WINNER'S CIRCLE
AT THE DAYTONA 500

RANDOM PAGES FROM A PETTY NOTEBOOK...

1971

1979

1981

1966

STP, Prestone and Simoniz.

Proud to be the official car care products of the Daytona 500 by STP.

DAYTONA 500 BY STP PRACTICE & QUALIFYING

By Tom Higgins

Ken Schrader could ride gloriously into NASCAR Winston Cup Series history by driving his Chevrolet to a fourth straight Daytona 500 pole position in the 1991 time trials for stock car racing's biggest event.

However, Schrader concededly is no historian and said before the race, "The record doesn't mean that much to me personally."

"I'd rather be a one-time Daytona 500 champion than a four-time winner of the pole," Schrader said during a break in practice, 24 hours before qualifying officially opens the stock car racing portion of Speed Weeks. "The pole doesn't pay much, and nothing extra for four in a row. However, Richard Broome, my crew chief, and the rest of the guys on the team have a tremendous desire to win this pole, so I'll try to hold my breath on one lap for them. The neatest thing about it for me would be that it

meant we beat everybody else this particular time."

Schrader shares the mark for three straight Busch Pole Awards in NASCAR's biggest event with Bill Elliott, who achieved the feat of topping time trials 1985-87, and the late Fireball Roberts, who did it 1961-63.

Unofficial clockings during practice indicated that Schrader and his Hendrick Motorsports team had a shot, with a lap at 193.594 mph. Fastest according to most timers under gray, chilly conditions were Davey Allison, Ford, 195.980; Harry Gant, Olds, 195.482; Michael Waltrip, Pontiac, 195.160; Ricky Rudd, Chevy, 194.864; and Ernie Irvan, Chevy, 194.594.

Rookie Robby Gordon, 21, proving that Daytona is more easily challenged than conquered, crashed the Junie Donlavey team's Ford in turn 4 in a late run. He was unhurt, but the car was heavily damaged, forcing

entry of a backup.

Most drivers predicted it would take 196 mph to earn the two front row spots, the only positions available.

"We had some laps we're happy with," continued Schrader. "And I think we'll be in the top three or four. I never know what Richard (Broome) is holding back on me in practice. Judging from what the stopwatches showed quite a few of 'em are going to run good. We're glad to be among the quickest, 'cause it's my feeling that you usually won't win the Daytona 500 unless you're fast enough to at least threaten to win the pole."

Schrader has had the most powerful car in the last two 500s. However, he finished as the runnerup in '89 when Darrell Waltrip won a gamble on gas mileage. Last February Schrader, forced to the rear of the field for the start when an accident dictated use of a backup Chevy (he was still cred-

Polesitter Davey Allison...can he stop Winston Cup champion Dale Earnhardt?

ited with the pole) passed 40 cars in a colossal charge before his engine soured. A crash in a 125 mile qualifying race brought the backup car into action.

Allison, fastest on practically all hand-held stopwatches operated by crewmen atop trucks in the garage area, expressed quiet confidence that the Schrader streak in qualifying could be severed.

"We pretty well know we can equal our practice laps in time trials if weather conditions are about the same," said the driver of the Robert Yates Racing team's Ford. "And we might even have a little bit left. I'm excited about our chances."

Ken Schrader failed in his gallant attempt at four consecutive Daytona 500 poles. Davey Allison lived up to his own predictions, captured the '91 pole and, along with it a special line in the Daytona 500 record book. He became the first second generation driver to win the coveted no. 1 starting position.

Driving the Robert Yates team's Charlotte-based Ford to a lap of 195.955 mph, Davey joined his legendary father, Bobby, as a 500 pole winner. The elder Allison, now a team owner, qualified a Pontiac fastest prior to the 1981 classic at the 2.5 mile track.

Schrader wound up eighth fastest at 194.045 mph in a Chevy, still within striking distance for the race itself.

Davey, who turns 30 on February 25, was the only driver to crack the 46 second mark with a time of 45.929. This enabled him to edge Chevrolet rival Ernie Irvan, clocked moments earlier at 46.003 seconds, or 195.639 mph, for the no.1 starting spot in the $2.5 million race. Irvan's lap gave him the other front row slot, as only the top two positions are locked in during first round time trials.

The remainder of the field will be determined in further time tri-

als later in the week, followed by two 125 mile qualifying races.

"Larry Wallace and the other guys in the engine room did a great job working out how to get more power from an engine with a restrictor plate," praised a grinning Allison, referring to the carburetor device that limits the flow of the air/fuel mixture to keep speeds down for safety's sake at Daytona and its sister track, Talladega Superspeedway. "And ol' Jake Elder gave me a perfect chassis. The car never quivered or slipped at any point on the track. The car drove perfect, I couldn't have asked for better. Today, we had the total package. It's a big kick for us, and maybe we can come back next week and get our first Daytona 500 victory."

Davey's best prior finish in the 500 was second—just behind his father in 1988.

Outside on the front row, looked good to Irvan. He bubbled, "I got a good lap in, the quickest we've had here. I'm definitely pleased. I guess my team (the Morgan/McClure operation) pulled something out for me. Davey was just too strong. He has been since we got here. We're proud to be the fastest Chevy."

Schrader took the end of his streak in stride. "That's all we had," said Schrader of his Hendrick Motorsports team, dismissing a suggestion that a wind which kicked up and blew directly down the backstretch slowed late qualifiers after Allison and Irvan went out early. "We hadn't practiced that fast or run that good since we got here."

"Unfortunately, I'm not in the Busch Clash tomorrow for 1990's pole winners," said Allison with a smile. "But now I'm already in it for 1992." Allison said "it was a killer of a time" waiting for all the powerful cars in line behind him to finish qualifying. "There were some guys back there like Ricky

Rudd and Kenny Schrader who make a habit of knocking people off provisional poles," said Allison.

As it turned out, neither of those drivers, generally favored to qualify fastest, came close. Rudd was seventh fastest, marginally quicker than eighth fastest Schrader.

Only one driver in line on pit road at the 2.5 mile track behind Allison was to top 195 and pose a threat. That was Harry Gant, who wound up third fastest in an Olds at 195.465 mph.

The only rival Allison, who was seventh in line for qualifying, had to beat, Ernie Irvan, went out fourth and ran 195.639.

Gant believes that he might have had a chance at the pole except for a scary experience during his run. "When I was coming off turn 2 an oil line must have blown off or maybe a plug wire came loose," said Gant. "Smoke started coming into the car and I lost my concentration. It got real bad in turns 3 and 4. It cost me some…I'm just glad that if it was oil, nothing got under my wheels."

Drivers with new teams, Sterling Marlin in a Ford and Rick Mast in an Olds, completed the top five. Winston Cup champion Dale Earnhardt was sixth and defending 500 champion Derrike Cope was 22nd, both in Chevys.

"We're staying consistent and that's what we want," said Earnhardt, timed at 194.368 mph. "That's what we want and we're right on the mark."

Seven-time Daytona 500 winner Richard Petty had his best qualifying run at the track in some time, placing 14th at 194.345 mph. "That's great, man," said Petty. "We psyched the fans up last year (by leading a 125 mile qualifying race) and we're going to excite them more this time. I think we're capable of winning again."

THE GATORADE 125 MILE QUALIFYING RACES

By Tom Higgins

Davey Allison and Dale Earnhardt both led all the way to win Gatorade 125 mile qualifying races leading to the Daytona 500, the NASCAR Winston Cup Series season opener.

The Ford-driving Allison, who locked up the pole position for the 500 the previous Saturday with a lap of 195.955 mph, outran the impressively strong Pontiac of a resurgent Richard Petty and the Buick of Hut Stricklin in the opening race, delayed four hours by rain. Petty, a seven-time Daytona 500 winner who hasn't triumphed since getting victory no. 200 on the famous Florida track in July of 1984, edged Stricklin in a photo finish. Stricklin's team is owned by Bobby Allison, Davey's dad.

Earnhardt enhanced his role as an overwhelming favorite in the 500, the sport's most important race, by nipping fellow Chevrolet driver Ernie Irvan and the Pontiac of Kyle Petty, Richard's son, as the second 50-lapper on the 2.5 mile track finished just before dark.

Time trials gave Irvan Sunday's other front row spot. Thursday's win put Earnhardt in position no. 3 for the 200 lap classic.

The top 14 finishers in each race, aside from Allison and Irvan, got positions 3-30 in the 500. The remainder of the field was determined by qualifying speeds and provisional starting opportunities.

A caution flag on lap 49 caused by a crash involving Sammy Swindell and Dorsey Schroeder, neither seriously hurt, kept Davey Allison from having to battle Richard Petty and Stricklin to the checkered flag. "If the yellow hadn't come out, I believe Hut could have given me all I could handle," Allison said of his cousin-by-marriage.

Brett Bodine crashed hard off turn 4 in the second race and appeared unhurt, but was taken to a local hospital for precautionary examination.

Said Earnhardt, who also won the Busch Clash special event last Sunday: "We were worried about making it all the way on fuel, but the caution laps due to Brett's wreck helped save gas. I feathered the throttle some, too, but not a lot. Ernie bothered me a bit the last lap when he hit me and almost got me sideways. He almost spun me out."

Allison wasn't passed once in taking the first of the twin 125 mile races.

"That's pretty impressive to me," conceded Allison. "But Dale Earnhardt led the second race all the way, and that's impressive, too."

As Allison won his first 125 under caution on the 49th of 50 laps, Petty, taking his Pontiac to the lowest line possible on the inside, edged Stricklin's Buick in a race back to the stripe for second place.

"I should have been able to drive away from them several times, but my car developed a push (understeer)," said Allison. "I saw them coming up on me late in the race, but I was going to be in their way."

Said Petty, who'll start on the second row in pursuit of an eighth Daytona 500 win: "I had to take a little bit of a chance going so low, but it worked out (as he and Stricklin passed a lapped car on opposite sides). I couldn't do anything with Davey. He was strong, but I think Hut maybe had the best car. I thought I could aggravate Davey to where he'd slip, but I couldn't catch him enough. Watch out. We may be there Sunday."

Said Stricklin: "Hopefully, we'll get a little more out of our motor Sunday. The car is handling so good, sticking right on the bottom, and I feel in a 500 mile race that'll be the key."

After winning a 125-miler a second straight year, and his fourth overall, Earnhardt predicted a very competitive Daytona 500. "It'll be interesting… one or two guys won't run off," said Earnhardt, who almost everyone expects to do just that after he led all 50 laps at the 2.5 mile track for his second triumph here in five days. He earlier overwhelmed the field in the Busch Clash special event. "But even if it is close, I feel confident we (the Richard Childress team fielding Earnhardt's Chevrolet) will be strong. All we're asking for is a shot, and I'm excited about the way the car is running."

Earnhardt appeared a bit upset about contact with Irvan on the last lap. He said Irvan almost spun him out with a bump from behind.

Said Irvan: "We got a good run at Dale and he pulled in front of me. I hit him, but nobody wrecked, so no harm done. Kyle was pushing on me and that made it a heck of a race. We've got a motor with a little more acceleration for the 500."

Said Kyle Petty, who watched his father, Richard, finish second to winner Davey Allison in the first race: "We were strong, but just didn't have enough to get by Dale and Ernie at the end. We've got a lot of stuff to try in the remaining practices. With the two Chevys running together in the draft, it was tough. I tried them with six laps to go and couldn't do it. My dad ran great. He beat my finish. Davey Allison ran good, but I was pulling for the King (Richard Petty) to come on up there and get around him."

It all matches. Winning Twin 125 Mile Qualifying Race drivers Dale Earnhardt and Davey Allison collect identical $35,000 checks, and Rolex watches, while flashing matching smiles in the Gatorade Winner's Circle.

FIRST GATORADE TWIN 125 MILE QUALIFYING RACE
February 14, 1991
OFFICIAL RESULTS

FIN POS	STR POS	CAR NO.	DRIVER	TEAM/CAR	LAPS	MONEY	STATUS
1	1	28	DAVEY ALLISON	Havoline Ford	50	$35,000	Running
2	7	43	RICHARD PETTY	STP Pontiac	50	22,000	Running
3	9	12	HUT STRICKLIN	Raybestos Buick	50	15,000	Running
4	3	1	RICK MAST	Skoal Classic Oldsmobile	50	10,000	Running
5	4	5	RICKY RUDD	Tide Chevrolet	50	8,000	Running
6	2	33	HARRY GANT	Skoal Bandit Oldsmobile	50	4,900	Running
7	10	30	MICHAEL WALTRIP	Pennzoil Pontiac	50	4,700	Running
8	6	9	BILL ELLIOTT	Coors Light Ford	50	4,550	Running
9	8	21	DALE JARRETT	Citgo Ford	50	4,400	Running
10	14	11	GEOFF BODINE	Budweiser Ford	50	4,150	Running
11	15	89	JIM SAUTER	Evinrude Pontiac	50	4,000	Running
12	13	98	JIMMY SPENCER	Banquet Frozen Food Chevrolet	50	3,850	Running
13	25	18	GREG SACKS	U.S. Navy Chevrolet	50	3,700	Running
14	5	7	ALAN KULWICKI	U.S. Army Ford	50	3,550	Running
15	16	73	PHIL BARKDOLL	X-1R Friction Elim. Oldsmobile	50	3,400	Running
16	11	10	DERRIKE COPE	Purolator Chevrolet	50	3,150	Running
17	12	24	MICKEY GIBBS	U.S. Air Force Pontiac	49	3,000	Running
18	18	55	TED MUSGRAVE*	U*S Racing Pontiac	49	2,850	Running
19	21	47	RICH BICKLE, JR.*	Kanawha Insurance Oldsmobile	49	2,700	Running
20	27	13	BRIAN ROSS	Interstate Lumber Buick	48	2,600	Running
21	23	80	JIMMY HORTON	Miles Concrete Chevrolet	48	2,400	Running
22	22	65	DAVE MADER*	Jasper Engines Chevrolet	48	2,300	Running
23	20	69	DORSEY SCHROEDER*	NAPA Auto Parts Ford	47	2,200	Accident
24	17	20	SAMMY SWINDELL*	Glad Bag Oldsmobile	47	2,100	Accident
25	29	45	PHILLIP DUFFIE	Fulcher Motorsports Oldsmobile	35	2,000	Handling
26	19	23	EDDIE BIERSCHWALE	Auto Finders Oldsmobile	24	1,900	Handling
27	24	27	BOBBY HILLIN	Moroso Racing Oldsmobile	18	2,300	Handling
28	28	0	DELMA COWART	Carey Hilliard's Rest. Chevrolet	18	1,750	Handling
29	26	82	MARK STAHL	Hooters Ford	10	1,650	Water Pump

TIME OF RACE: 00:45:21
AVERAGE SPEED: 165.380 mph
MARGIN OF VICTORY: finished under caution

CAUTION FLAGS: 2 flags for 5 laps
LEAD CHANGES: 0
*NASCAR Winston Cup Rookie of the Year Candidate

Richard Petty's bold late stage move in the STP Pontiac earned him second place to winner Davey Allison in the first Twin 125 Qualifying Race, good for third place on the starting grid of the Daytona 500.

First at the start, first at the finish 50 laps later, Davey Allison was the clear-cut winner of the first Twin 125 Qualifying Race, solidifying the pole position he had already won for the Daytona 500 and reinforcing his role as one of the favorites for the "main event".

SECOND GATORADE TWIN 125 MILE QUALIFYING RACE
February 14, 1991
OFFICIAL RESULTS

FIN POS	STR POS	CAR NO.	DRIVER	TEAM/CAR	LAPS	MONEY	STATUS
1	3	3	DALE EARNHARDT	GM Goodwrench Chevrolet	50	$35,000	Running
2	1	4	ERNIE IRVAN	Kodak Film Chevrolet	50	22,000	Running
3	10	42	KYLE PETTY	Mello Yello Pontiac	50	15,000	Running
4	8	2	RUSTY WALLACE	Miller Genuine Draft Pontiac	50	10,000	Running
5	5	17	DARRELL WALTRIP	Western Auto Chevrolet	50	8,000	Running
6	2	22	STERLING MARLIN	Maxwell House Coffee Ford	50	4,900	Running
7	6	75	JOE RUTTMAN	Dinner Bell Foods Oldsmobile	50	4,700	Running
8	21	88	BUDDY BAKER	U.S. Marines Pontiac	50	4,550	Running
9	4	6	MARK MARTIN	Folgers Coffee Ford	50	4,400	Running
10	13	68	BOBBY HAMILTON*	Country Time Drink Oldsmobile	50	4,150	Running
11	25	51	JEFF PURVIS	Plasti-Kote Oldsmobile	50	4,000	Running
12	16	25	KEN SCHRADER	Kodiak Chevrolet	50	3,850	Running
13	19	8	RICK WILSON	SNICKERS Buick	50	3,700	Running
14	9	66	DICK TRICKLE	TropArtic Pontiac	50	3,550	Running
15	12	19	CHAD LITTLE	Bull's Eye BBQ Ford	50	3,400	Running
16	17	90	ROBBY GORDON	Publix Supermarkets Ford	50	3,150	Running
17	18	52	JIMMY MEANS	Alka-Seltzer Pontiac	50	3,000	Running
18	7	94	TERRY LABONTE	Sunoco Oldsmobile	50	2,850	Running
19	15	95	RICK JEFFREY	Kentucky Fried Chicken Chevrolet	50	2,700	Running
20	22	34	GARY BALOUGH	Allen's Assoc. Glass Chevrolet	50	2,600	Running
21	27	70	J. D. MCDUFFIE	Run-A-Bout Pontiac	50	2,400	Running
22	23	96	PHIL PARSONS	Los Gatos Ferrari Chevrolet	49	2,300	Running
23	26	35	BILL VENTURINI	Amoco Ultimate Chevrolet	48	2,200	Running
24	20	72	CHUCK BOWN	Tex Racing Oldsmobile	48	2,100	Running
25	28	99	BRAD TEAGUE	Traffic Engineering Chevrolet	35	2,000	Engine
26	14	71	DAVE MARCIS	U.S. Coast Guard Chevrolet	31	1,900	Wheel Bear.
27	24	26	BRETT BODINE	Quaker State Buick	21	2,300	Accident
28	29	39	BLACKIE WANGERIN	Wangerin Racing Ford	6	1,750	Handling
29	11	15	MORGAN SHEPHERD	Motorcraft Ford	1	1,650	Engine

TIME OF RACE: 00:47:50
AVERAGE SPEED: 156.794 mph
MARGIN OF VICTORY: 1 car length

CAUTION FLAGS: 1 flag for 7 laps
LEAD CHANGES: 1 lead change, 2 drivers
*NASCAR Winston Cup Rookie of the Year Candidate

THE MEN OF THE 500

Starting 1st
DAVEY ALLISON, Car No. 28
Havoline Ford, Speed 195.955

Starting 2nd
ERNIE IRVAN, Car No. 4
Kodak Film Chevrolet, Speed 195.639

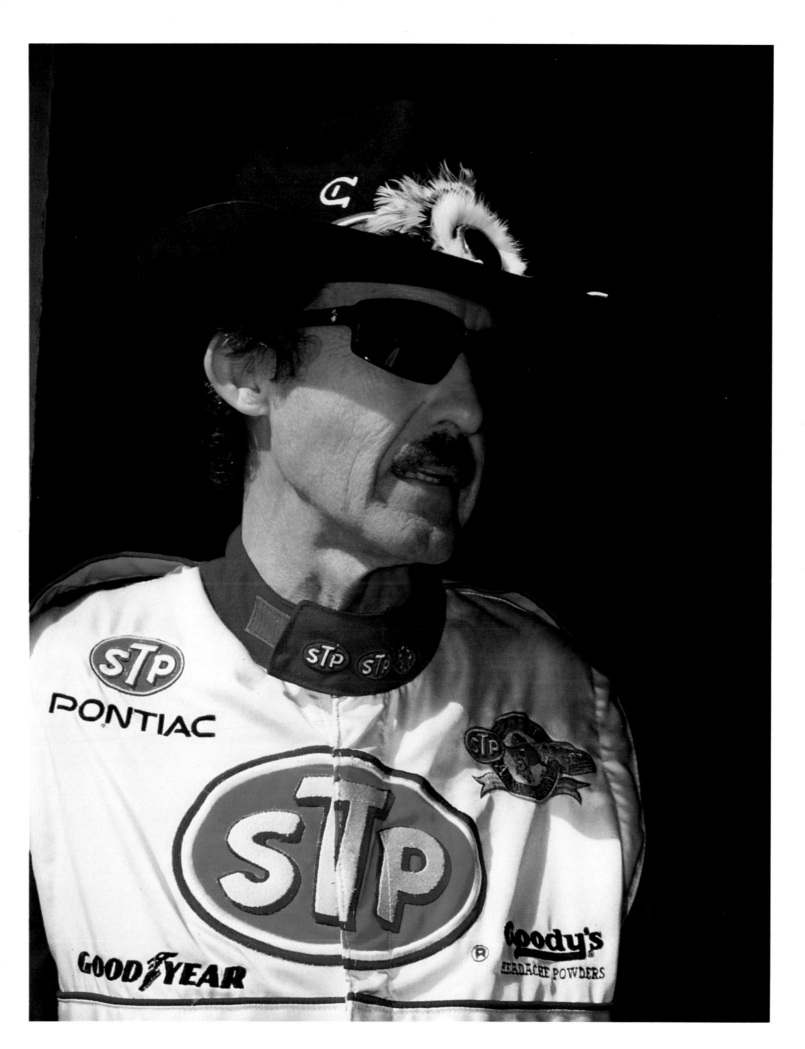

Starting 3rd
RICHARD PETTY, Car No. 43
STP Pontiac, 2nd, Qualifying Race No. 1

Starting 4th
DALE EARNHARDT, Car No. 3
GM Goodwrench Chevrolet, 1st, Qualifying
Race No. 2

Starting 5th
HUT STRICKLIN, Car No. 12
Raybestos Buick, 3rd, Qualifying Race No. 1

Starting 6th
KYLE PETTY, Car No. 42
Mello Yello Pontiac, 3rd, Qualifying Race No. 2

Starting 7th
RICK MAST, Car No. 1
Skoal Classic Oldsmobile, 4th, Qualifying
Race No. 1

Starting 8th
RUSTY WALLACE, Car No. 2
Miller Genuine Draft Pontiac, 4th, Qualifying
Race No. 2

Starting 9th
RICKY RUDD, Car No. 5
Tide Chevrolet, 5th, Qualifying Race No. 1

Starting 10th
DARRELL WALTRIP, Car No. 17
Western Auto Chevrolet, 5th, Qualifying
Race No. 2

Starting 11th
HARRY GANT, Car No. 33
Skoal Bandit Oldsmobile, 6th, Qualifying
Race No. 1

Starting 12th
STERLING MARLIN, Car No. 22
Maxwell House Coffee Ford, 6th, Qualifying
Race No. 2

Starting 13th
MICHAEL WALTRIP, Car No. 30
Pennzoil Pontiac, 7th, Qualifying Race No. 1

Starting 14th
JOE RUTTMAN, Car No. 75
Dinner Bell Foods Oldsmobile, 7th, Qualifying
Race No. 2

Starting 15th
BILL ELLIOTT, Car No. 9
Coors Light Ford, 8th, Qualifying Race No. 1

Starting 16th
BUDDY BAKER, Car No. 88
U.S. Marines Pontiac, 8th, Qualifying Race No. 2

Starting 17th
DALE JARRETT, Car No. 21
Citgo Ford, 9th, Qualifying Race No. 1

Starting 18th
MARK MARTIN, Car No. 6
Folgers Coffee Ford, 9th, Qualifying Race No. 2

Starting 19th
GEOFF BODINE, Car No. 11
Budweiser Ford, 10th, Qualifying Race No. 1

Starting 20th
BOBBY HAMILTON, Car No. 68*
Country Time Drink Mix Oldsmobile, 10th,
Qualifying Race No. 2

Starting 21st
JIM SAUTER, Car No. 89
Evinrude Pontiac, 11th, Qualifying Race No. 1

Starting 22nd
JEFF PURVIS, Car No. 51
Plasti-Kote Oldsmobile, 11th, Qualifying
Race No. 2

Starting 23rd
JIMMY SPENCER, Car No. 98
Banquet Frozen Foods Chevrolet, 12th,
Qualifying Race No. 1

Starting 25th
GREG SACKS, Car No. 18
U.S. Navy Chevrolet, 13th, Qualifying Race No. 1

Starting 24th
KEN SCHRADER, Car No. 25
Kodiak Chevrolet, 12th, Qualifying Race No. 2

Starting 26th
RICK WILSON, Car No. 8
SNICKERS Buick, 13th, Qualifying Race No. 2

Starting 28th
DICK TRICKLE, Car No. 66
TropArtic Pontiac, 14th, Qualifying Race No. 2

Starting 27th
ALAN KULWICKI, Car No. 7
U.S. Army Ford, 14th, Qualifying Race No. 1

Starting 30th
CHAD LITTLE, Car No. 19
Bull's Eye BBQ Sauce Ford, 15th, Qualifying
Race No. 2

Starting 31st
TERRY LABONTE, Car No. 94
Sunoco Oldsmobile, Speed 193.228

Starting 33rd
DERRIKE COPE, Car No. 10
Purolator Chevrolet, Speed 192.336

Starting 32nd
SAMMY SWINDELL, Car No. 20
GLAD Bag Oldsmobile, Speed 192.740

Starting 34th
MORGAN SHEPHERD, Car No. 15
Motorcraft Ford, Speed 192.254

Starting 35th
ROBBY GORDON, Car No. 90
Publix Supermarkets Ford, Speed 192.238

Starting 36th
BOBBY HILLIN, Car No. 27
Moroso Racing Oldsmobile, Speed 192.160

Starting 37th
TED MUSGRAVE, Car No. 55*
U*S Racing Pontiac, Speed 192.127

Starting 38th
MICKEY GIBBS, Car No. 24
U.S. Air Force Pontiac, Speed 192.053

Starting 39th
JIMMY MEANS, Car No. 52
Alka-Seltzer Pontiac, Speed 191.697

Starting 40th
EDDIE BIERSCHWALE, Car No. 23
Auto Finders Oldsmobile, Speed 191.608

Starting 41st
BRETT BODINE, Car No. 26
Quaker State Buick, Provisional Starting
Position

Starting 42nd
DAVE MARCIS, Car No. 71
U.S. Coast Guard Chevrolet, Provisional Starting
Position

*NASCAR Winston Cup Rookie of the Year Candidate

Starting positions 1 and 2 based on speeds attained on the first day of official qualifications, positions 3 through 30 on results of Twin 125 Mile
Qualifying races. Positions 31 through 40 based on qualifying speeds. Two provisional starting positions based on 1990 Winston Cup Car Owner
Point Standings. Users of back-up cars moved to back of the field.

DAYTONA™ 500

The Men and Machines of Speed Weeks '90

Big 160 page, 9" x 12" hardcover book with full coverage of every Speed Weeks racing event in color, including every Daytona 500 qualifier, special reports on Derrike Cope, Richard Petty, and the movie "Days of Thunder".

COLLECTOR'S EDITION

Please send me _____ copies of
Daytona 500, The Men and Machines of Speed Weeks '90
at **$19.95 each plus $2.00 shipping**
I enclose check or money order payable to:
AUTOSPORT INTERNATIONAL, INC.,
79 Madison Avenue, Suite 1200,
New York, New York, 10016, (212) 689-8086

NAME:_____

STREET ADDRESS:_____

CITY:_____ STATE:_____ ZIP CODE:_____

//NASCAR

Pontiac pace cars get the Daytona 500 off to a smooth, swift start.

Start of the Daytona 500 by STP brings packed stands to their feet and cheering.

DAYTONA 500 BY STP

ERNIE IRVAN WINS UNDER CAUTION, EARNHARDT DENIED AGAIN

By Tom Higgins

Ernie Irvan, his Chevrolet almost out of fuel and sputtering although running slow under caution conditions, won a Daytona 500 by STP that turned bizarre as three accidents altered the outcome in the last 40 miles. "I felt my car running out of gas while leading under the last yellow flag with still about a lap to go," Irvan said after the stunning finish in the NASCAR Winston Cup Series season opener. "I said, 'This can't be true. This can't happen to me.'"

It didn't, quite, but runnerup Sterling Marlin, alongside Irvan in a Ford, thought it might. "Ernie's car was sputtering so bad when we got to turns 3 and 4 that I thought it was going to stop," said Marlin. "I was saying, Quit! Quit! Quit!' But it didn't."

Joe Ruttman, driving an Olds, finished third on the lead lap in a race in which new pit rules kept the top contenders strung out far apart much of the way.

Rick Mast was fourth in an Oldsmobile, followed in fifth by pre-race favorite Dale Earnhardt's

Chevrolet, the dominant car and driver combination in pre-500 Speed Weeks events.

The race's twists and turns also left Earnhardt, Darrell Waltrip, Davey Allison, Rusty Wallace, and Kyle Petty muttering "This can't be happening."

At the final rundown, for the second time in three years, it appeared that Waltrip would win stock car racing's premier event by getting superior gas mileage in his Chevy.

Waltrip was running third and positioned to go the distance on the 2.5 mile track with 16 laps left while Allison and Wallace, one-two at the time, faced pitting for fuel. No one behind Waltrip was close enough to catch him.

When Richard Petty and Robby Gordon spun on the 184th of the race's 200 laps and forced a yellow flag, however, Waltrip's edge was erased. His rivals were able to pit for enough gas to finish.

The field bunched for the restart on lap 189 in this order: Wallace, Waltrip, Earnhardt, Irvan, Kyle Petty, Mast, Ruttman,

Marlin, and Derrike Cope. Earnhardt surged ahead in turn 3, followed by Irvan.

Behind them, the Pontiacs of Kyle Petty and Wallace touched, entering the homestretch, triggering a crash that damaged the Wallace, Waltrip, Cope, Hut Stricklin and Harry Gant cars. Again, the yellow flag showed.

Earnhardt led the restart on lap 194, but Irvan whipped by going into turn 1 on lap 195 and pulled away to a five car length lead as Earnhardt and Allison raced abreast behind him.

On lap 198, Earnhardt's car went out of control off turn 2, sweeping both Allison and Kyle Petty into a wreck. This created yet another caution period and with just two laps left, not enough to clear the wreckage in time to put the field back under green, Irvan was home free under the yellow flag. If he had enough gas. He did. Barely.

While Irvan and his Morgan/ McClure Racing teammates celebrated in victory lane after making the sport's biggest show their

second Winston Cup triumph, rivals lamented the wrecks that crushed their chances.

"The race was ours just to drive into victory circle," said Waltrip, making his first start for the new DarWal Inc., team that he owns. "It was no problem if it hadn't been for that wreck (Richard Petty and Gordon). Why did we have to have that caution? Nobody could have run me down if the race had gone green the rest of the way. I know I could have made it without stopping for fuel."

Petty commiserated with Waltrip. "I got behind Harry Gant coming off turn 2 and the air from his car made mine break loose. It made a couple of wiggles heading to the infield, then came back across the track, spun the wrong way and got busted up pretty good."

Kyle Petty's attempted pass of Wallace triggered the next incident. "I guess Kyle didn't see me and drifted up in front of my car," said Wallace. "We ran out of room in a hurry. I thought I was going to finish third at worst and maybe win because we had enough fuel to finish, too, just like Darrell."

Said Kyle Petty: "I know Rusty is disappointed. A lot of us are. It wasn't intentional."

Like Richard Petty, Earnhardt traced a loss of aerodynamics to the spin that took out Allison and the younger Petty. "I lost control when the wind came off my rear spoiler," said Earnhardt. "That spun me up into Davey. Luckily, I was able to come on around and not lose any laps. I was hoping Davey would stay behind me and we'd get back by Ernie one way or another and then race for it ourselves, but he wouldn't give me any room."

Allison had a different view of the accident that left him with a 15th place finish. "I got hit in the left side and it put me in the wall," said Allison. "I was passing him clean on the outside and I got hit and I ain't happy. Dale has got everybody so scared right now no one would draft with me. We had the horsepower to win if I could have gotten around without that incident."

Later, after watching tape replays, Allison agreed that Earnhardt's car lost traction because of aerodynamic factors, not a move by the driver.

"I saw the smoke from the mess between Dale and Davey and Kyle in my mirror and sensed what had happened," said Irvan. "I knew the yellow had to come out, and I told myself, 'Don't let off the throttle or somebody will come boiling by and beat you back to the line.'"

But no rival had enough steam to do that, and the bright yellow Kodak-backed Chevrolet inched its way into victory circle to face a platoon of eager photographers.

Dale denied again. Dale Earnhardt shown with Kirk Shelmerdine and wife Teresa, dismayed the Winston Cup contingent by sweeping all the preliminaries with ease. Once again, the Daytona "main event" eluded the 1990 Winston Cup titlist, despite a strong run.

Polesitter Davey Allison's Havoline Ford was in contention all the way, until an accident involving Earnhardt three laps from the finish ended his fine run.

Darrell Waltrip in the Western Auto Chevrolet was in good strategic position for a charge to the finish when an accident ended his day.

Dominant in all the 500 preliminaries, Dale Earnhardt had his Goodwrench Chevrolet in the lead on laps 189-194 late in the race, was outgunned by Ernie Irvan on a restart. He's shown with Kyle Petty in the Mello Yello Pontiac, who was involved in an accident induced when Earnhardt tried to regain the lead. The third car shown is Ricky Rudd's Tide Chevrolet, the eventual 9th place finisher.

THE MACHINES OF THE 500

Drivers of the U.S. Armed Services entries, made possible by R. J. Reynolds, accept an emotional pre-race salute from Daytona's packed stands. From the left, Mickey Gibbs in the Air Force Pontiac, Greg Sacks in the Navy Chevrolet, Alan Kulwicki in the Army Ford, Buddy Baker in the Marines Pontiac, and Dave Marcis in the Coast Guard Chevrolet.

Sterling Marlin, in the Maxwell House Ford, avoided all the late race incidents which claimed other leading contenders, finished second from his twelfth place starting position.

Bobby Hamilton pit stop

Jimmy Spencer bails out of his hot seat in a crashed and burning Chevrolet.

Dale Jarrett, in the Citgo Ford, improved his position steadily from the 17th slot on the starting grid, took down sixth place. Michael Waltrip's day in the Pennzoil Pontiac ended early with mechanical problems.

Veteran Phil Barkdoll, in his own Oldsmobile, recovered from this awkward stance to finish 20th.

Close quarters, too close, put 1990 winner Derrike Cope in the Purolator Chevrolet out of contention, along with Hut Stricklin in the Raybestos Buick, and Harry Gant in the Skoal Bandit Oldsmobile before the race reached its critical final stage.

Friend and foe...A sea of friendly spectator faces stretches beyond the forbidding concrete wall of Daytona's trioval.

Dale Earnhardt's polished Goodwrench crew turned in another of their virtuoso performances, this one to no avail when a late race accident demoted their charger to a fifth place finish.

Final Four...Davey Allison, Dale Earnhardt, Ernie Irvan, and Kyle Petty in close company in the final stages. At the end it was Irvan, all alone.

THE MACHINES OF THE 500

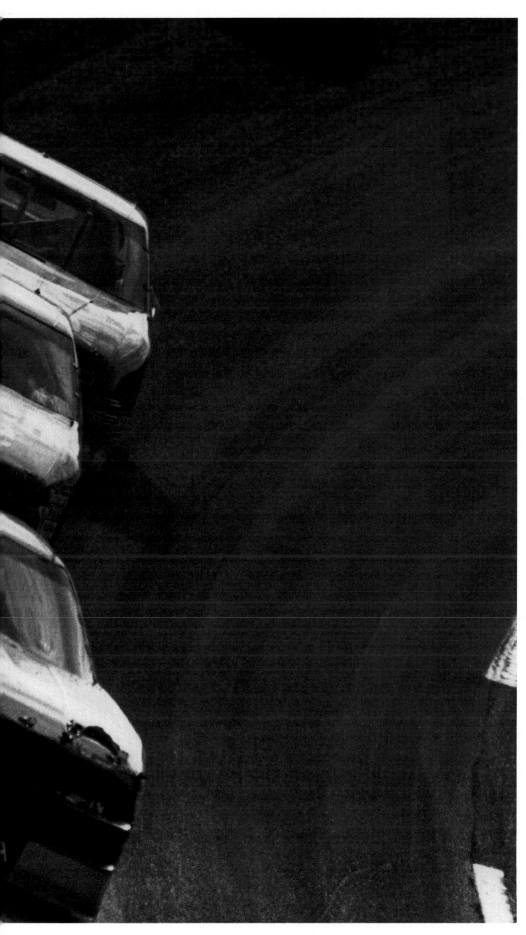

Dale Earnhardt in the Goodwrench Chevrolet slips sideways, taps Davey Allison as the race nears its highly unusual end. Both lost their chances at the victory. Joe Ruttman in the Dinner Bell Oldsmobile and Sterling Marlin in the Maxwell House Ford, immediately behind this pair, escape the tangle.

Ruttman and Marlin futilely pursue leader Ernie Irvan in the low on fuel Kodak Chevrolet under yellow all the way to the finish line.

Ernie Irvan's Kodak Chevrolet crosses the finish stripe for the checker in one of the most bizarre 500s on record.

First ever Daytona 500 by STP trophy goes to winner Ernie Irvan. First Brands Chairman and CEO Al Dudley does the honors.

DAYTONA 500 BY STP
Daytona International Speedway
Daytona Beach, Florida—2.5 Mile High-Banked, Asphalt Speedway
February 17, 1991—500 M—200 L—Purse $2,181,370

FIN POS	STR POS	CAR NO	DRIVER	TEAM	LAPS	WINSTON CUP POINTS	BONUS POINTS	TOTAL MONEY WON	STATUS
1	2	4	ERNIE IRVAN	Kodak Film Chevrolet	200	180*	5	$233,000	Running
2	12	22	STERLING MARLIN	Maxwell House Coffee Ford	200	175*	5	133,925	Running
3	14	75	JOE RUTTMAN	Dinner Bell Foods Oldsmobile	200	170*	5	111,450	Running
4	7	1	RICK MAST	Skoal Classic Oldsmobile	200	165*	5	100,900	Running
5	4	3	DALE EARNHARDT	GM Goodwrench Chevrolet	200	160*	5	113,850	Running
6	17	21	DALE JARRETT	Citgo Ford	199	150		74,900	Running
7	36	27	BOBBY HILLIN	Moroso Racing Oldsmobile	199	146		50,925	Running
8	27	7	ALAN KULWICKI	U.S. Army Ford	199	142		52,450	Running
9	9	5	RICKY RUDD	Tide Chevrolet	199	138		52,600	Running
10	20	68	BOBBY HAMILTON#	Country Time Drink Mix Olds	199	134		43,500	Running
11	28	66	DICK TRICKLE	TropArtic Pontiac	199	130		39,525	Running
12	40	23	EDDIE BIERSCHWALE	Auto Finders Oldsmobile	199	127		31,550	Running
13	31	94	TERRY LABONTE	Sunoco Oldsmobile	198	124		34,355	Running
14	30	19	CHAD LITTLE	Bull's Eye Barbecue Sauce Ford	198	121		29,540	Running
15	1	28	DAVEY ALLISON	Havoline Ford	197	123*	5	77,350	Accident
16	6	42	KYLE PETTY	Mello Yello Pontiac	197	125*	10	41,580	Accident
17	38	24	MICKEY GIBBS	U.S. Air Force Pontiac	197	112		24,560	Running
18	35	90	ROBBY GORDON	Publix Supermarkets Ford	196	109		23,740	Running
19	3	43	RICHARD PETTY	STP Pontiac	195	106		43,120	Running
20	29	73	PHIL BARKDOLL	Barkdoll Racing Oldsmobile	194	103		24,160	Running
21	18	6	MARK MARTIN	Folgers Coffee Ford	193	100		31,955	Running
22	41	26	BRETT BODINE	Quaker State Buick	193	97		23,400	Running
23	21	89	JIM SAUTER	Evinrude Pontiac	192	94		21,845	Running
24	10	17	DARRELL WALTRIP	Western Auto Chevrolet	190	96*	5	25,440	Accident
25	11	33	HARRY GANT	Skoal Bandit Oldsmobile	190	88		26,385	Accident
26	33	10	DERRIKE COPE	Purolator Chevrolet	189	85		28,180	Accident
27	8	2	RUSTY WALLACE	Miller Genuine Draft Pontiac	188	87*	5	26,425	Accident
28	15	9	BILL ELLIOTT	Coors Light Ford	188	79		28,670	Running
29	5	12	HUT STRICKLIN	Raybestos Buick	185	76		33,865	Accident
30	37	55	TED MUSGRAVE#	U*S Racing Pontiac	180	73		18,710	Running
31	24	25	KEN SCHRADER	Kodiak Chevrolet	176	70		22,330	Running
32	19	11	GEOFF BODINE	Budweiser Ford	150	67		28,150	Oil Leak
33	26	8	RICK WILSON	SNICKERS Buick	137	64		21,545	Running
34	34	15	MORGAN SHEPHERD	Motorcraft Ford	70	61		23,490	Piston
35	42	71	DAVE MARCIS	U.S. Coast Guard Chevrolet	40	58		19,185	Valve
36	22	51	JEFF PURVIS	Plasti-Kote Oldsmobile	37	55		18,380	Overheating
37	16	88	BUDDY BAKER	U.S. Marines Pontiac	35	52		18,800	Engine
38	13	30	MICHAEL WALTRIP	Pennzoil Pontiac	35	49		21,520	Piston
39	39	52	JIMMY MEANS	Alka-Seltzer Pontiac	29	46		17,660	Accident
40	23	98	JIMMY SPENCER	Banquet Frozen Foods Chevrolet	29	43		20,200	Accident
41	32	20	SAMMY SWINDELL#	Glad Bag Oldsmobile	28	40		16,500	Accident
42	25	18	GREG SACKS	U.S. Navy Chevrolet	20	37		17,450	Accident

TIME OF RACE: 3 hours, 22 minutes, 30 seconds   **AVERAGE SPEED:** 148.148 mph   **MARGIN OF VICTORY:** Under Caution
BUSCH POLE AWARD: Davey Allison, Havoline Ford, 195.955 mph (45.929 seconds)
BUSCH FASTEST SECOND-ROUND QUALIFIER: Phil Barkdoll, Barkdoll Racing Oldsmobile
RIGHT GUARD HALF-WAY CHALLENGE AWARD: Rick Mast, Skoal Classic Oldsmobile
TRUE VALUE HARD CHARGER AWARD: Kyle Petty, Mello Yello Pontiac (Allison, Earnhardt, Irvan, Mast)
GATORADE CIRCLE OF CHAMPIONS AWARD: Ernie Irvan, Kodak Film Chevrolet
TYSON LICKETY SPLIT AWARD: Dale Earnhardt, GM Goodwrench Chevrolet, 194.217 mph—lap 7
MICHIGAN/MC CORD ENGINE BUILDER OF THE RACE: Shelton Pittman, Kodak Film Chevrolet
PLASTI-KOTE WINNING FINISH AWARD: Tony Glover, Kodak Film Chevrolet
DINNER BELL TOP DOG AWARD: Ernie Irvan, Kodak Film Chevrolet
WESTERN AUTO MECHANIC OF THE RACE: Tony Glover, Kodak Film Chevrolet
BUDGET TEAM SERVICE AWARD: Morgan/McClure Racing
GOODY'S HEADACHE AWARD: Dale Earnhardt, GM Goodwrench Chevrolet
CAUTION FLAGS: 9 for 36 laps (15-17, 22-26, 32-35, 38-41, 69-74, 78-81, 185-188, 190-193, 199-200)
LAP LEADERS: Davey Allison 1, Dale Earnhardt 2-13, Allison 14-26, Earnhardt 27-32, Kyle Petty 33-36, Sterling Marlin 37-38, K. Petty 39-42, Earnhardt 43-64, Joe Ruttman 65-74, Allison 75-84, Marlin 85-89, Rick Mast 90-103, K. Petty 104-123, Ruttman 124, Ernie Irvan 125-133, Darrell Waltrip 134-146, K. Petty 147-169, Irvan 170-183, Allison 184-185, Rusty Wallace 186-188, Earnhardt 189-194, Irvan 195-200. 21 lead changes among 9 drivers. *Includes race leader/most laps bonus. #NASCAR Winston Cup Rookie of the Year challenger.

TOP 10 WINSTON CUP POINTS (WINS)

1-Ernie Irvan	180	(1)	6-Dale Jarrett	150	(0)
2-Sterling Marlin	175	(0)	7-Bobby Hillin	146	(0)
3-Joe Ruttman	170	(0)	8-Alan Kulwicki	142	(0)
4-Rick Mast	165	(0)	9-Ricky Rudd	138	(0)
5-Dale Earnhardt	160	(0)	10-Bobby Hamilton	134	(0)

DINNER BELL TOP DOG AWARD
Ernie Irvan   1

MANUFACTURERS CHAMPIONSHIP

	POINTS	WINS
Chevrolet	9	1
Ford	6	0
Oldsmobile	4	0
Pontiac	3	0
Buick	2	0

BUDGET TEAM SERVICE AWARD

Morgan/McClure Racing	(4)	180
Junior Johnson & Assoc.	(22)	175
Rohman Racing	(75)	170
Precision Products Racing	(1)	165
Wood Brothers Racing	(21)	150

TRUE VALUE HARD CHARGER

Kyle Petty	1115
Davey Allison	1048
Dale Earnhardt	1045
Ernie Irvan	920
Rick Mast	695

MICHIGAN/MC CORD ENGINE BUILDER OF THE YEAR

Shelton Pittman	(4)	15
Beecher Hetland	(22)	14
Dick Rahilly	(75)	13
Claude Queen	(1)	12
Ed Lanier	(3)	11

UNOCAL 76 POINT FUND STANDINGS

Ernie Irvan	180
Sterling Marlin	175
Joe Ruttman	170

GATORADE CIRCLE OF CHAMPIONS
Ernie Irvan   180

SEARS DIEHARD RACER MILES

Sterling Marlin	500.00
Joe Ruttman	500.00
Rick Mast	500.00
Dale Jarrett	497.50
Bobby Hillin	497.50

TYSON LICKETY SPLIT AWARD

Dale Earnhardt	25
Ernie Irvan	10
Davey Allison	10

NASCAR WINSTON CUP ROOKIE OF THE YEAR

Bobby Hamilton	12
Ted Musgrave	10
Sammy Swindell	9

BUSCH BEER POLE STANDINGS
Davey Allison   1

WESTERN AUTO MECHANIC OF THE YEAR

Tony Glover	(4)	29
Bob Johnson	(1)	27
Bob Rahilly	(75)	25
Jake Elder	(28)	25
Waddell Wilson	(5)	23

PLASTI-KOTE QUALITY FINISH AWARD

Tony Glover	(4)	1
Mike Beam	(22)	2
Bob Rahilly	(75)	3
Bob Johnson	(1)	4
Kirk Shelmerdine	(3)	5

Home free. Winner Ernie Irvan and his Kodak Chevrolet crew bask in the flash of photographers' bulbs as they take firm possession of victory circle.

ERNIE IRVAN

FROM WELDING RACING STANDS TO FILLING THEM IN FIVE SHORT YEARS

By Tom Higgins

As he blazed off turn 4 with six laps to go in the Daytona 500 by STP Ernie Irvan was faced with a split second decision. A win/lose decision.

Just ahead of him in the lead at Daytona International Speedway was Dale Earnhardt, going for a sweep of four NASCAR races in eight days at the 2.5 mile track.

"I didn't know whether to stay in Dale's draft or try to pass him, since it seemed I had a good shot," Irvan said. "Something told me to go ahead and get around him, and it was history after that."

'History' will show that Irvan, 32, a native of Salinas, CA, who moved to Concord, NC, in 1982 to pursue a Southern-style stock car racing career, led the rest of the way to win the sport's biggest event in only his third try. The triumph was only the second ever on the Winston Cup circuit for Irvan and his Morgan/McClure Racing team of Abingdon, VA. Owned by Larry McClure and led by crew chief Tony Glover and engine builder Shelton "Runt" Pittman, the team was ecstatic. Their first victory came in August of 1990 in the Busch 500 at Bristol (Tennessee) Raceway.

"After I got around Dale, I was looking in the rearview mirror more than straight ahead," confessed Irvan.

What he saw was fellow Chevrolet driver Earnhardt and Ford-mounted Allison battling abreast about five car lengths behind him. On lap 198 of the event's 200 laps, the swirl of air created in side-by-side racing caused Earnhardt's car to lose traction in turn 2 and he spun. Allison was swept into the Earnhardt miscue, along with Kyle Petty in a Pontiac.

"Dale, who is my hero, and Davey were doing the same thing back there that I'd have done in their position," said Irvan, who fortuitously overcame a stop-and-go penalty for driving above the traffic blend-in line while leaving the pits early in the race. "They were trying to win the race. I knew that if they stayed like that, I was in good shape, though. It meant they weren't lining up to draft by me."

Irvan, who got the competitive Morgan/McClure ride four races into the '90 season, was incredulous when told that he'd earned $233,000, the second largest purse in NASCAR history, without having to face a final lap restart. Not all of Irvan's luck has been as good, "I remember not too many years back when I didn't have a regular ride, Ken Schrader (another winning Chevy driver) moved to Concord and got me to help him unload his truck," said Irvan. "Kenny gave me $50 for the work, or I couldn't have eaten that week."

Irvan shook his head as other memories returned of how rough and uncertain the road had been enroute to the winner's circle in stock car racing's most important event. In an often touching post-race winner's interview Irvan recounted some mileposts on his road to instant celebrity.

He began racing in California at 16, driving a Chevelle he and his father, Vic, teamed to build. He won one of five races. In 1977, Irvan took the Stockton (California) Speedway track championship, winning 15 of 23 features.

Father Vic, who had competed on NASCAR's Winston West tour, moved to Concord in 1978 to go racing Down South. Ernie chose to stay in California, racing successfully on short tracks in the Modesto area. For the younger Irvan, like most other drivers his age, the chance of competing at the Winston Cup level was an almost constant challenge. Finally, the lure became overpowering, and Ernie moved across the continent to be nearer the Charlotte area, the big-time circuit's hub.

Ernie began competing almost immediately at Concord Motor Speedway, a half-mile track similar to those he'd run in California. He won the national championship for six cylinder cars there in '84, plus nine other races. The next season produced ten victories at Concord and '86 produced eight more, including three major triumphs. The '87 season yielded ten wins at Concord and Tri-County Speedway at Hudson, NC.

The swarthy, stocky driver's fullbore driving style and lack of fear in making contact on the track, a throwback to the sport's early days, earned him a nickname among local fans: "Swervin' Irvan".

His succession of trips to victory lane also was beginning to attract attention, and during the last third of the '87 Winston Cup season car owner/engineer Marc Reno fielded a Chevy for Irvan in five races. His first start on the senior circuit came on September 13 in the Wrangler 400 at Richmond (Virginia) Raceway. Irvan's car was sponsored by a Chevrolet dealership—the one owned by Dale Earnhardt.

D.K. Ulrich hired Irvan to drive for his U.S. Racing operation in 1988. He listed an 11th place at Martinsville (Virginia) Speedway as his best finish. After an excruciatingly close chase, he lost the rookie of the year title to Ken Bouchard by three points, a hint of things to come.

Irvan remained with Ulrich in '89, started all 29 races and notched four top 10 finishes, with a sixth at Martinsville as the best. Notably, in a stirring charge, he led the Busch 500 at Bristol for a considerable distance until a cut tire caused him to wreck in turn 4. That performance attracted a lot more attention.

Irvan was signed to take over the Fords of NASCAR veteran Junie Donlavey, who appeared to have a solid sponsor set for the '90 tour. However, the backing didn't develop. After three races Irvan found himself out of a ride and with no immediate prospects of another. "It was a terrible letdown…Junie is such a wonderful man and he was just crushed, as much for me as for himself," said Irvan.

Donlavey readily released Irvan when Larry McClure decided to make a driver change after just three races and offered his opening to Ernie.

"When it looked like I wasn't going to get to race, it brought back memories of some tough times," Irvan went on. "I remembered '85, and watching Bill Elliott win the Winston Million at Darlington and wishing I could be there. I was watching at my mobile home in Concord on a borrowed 14 inch, black and white television. Racing against Bill and the other Winston Cup guys seemed as far away as the stars. Later I got a job at Charlotte Motor Speedway when the construction was underway on one of its expansions. I was welding in new seats. It was agonizing being up there with that welder when there were cars out on the track for testing or practice. It nearly broke my heart." At this point, Irvan chuckled. "One good thing came of that odd job I took helping Kenny Schrader unload his truck," continued Irvan. "He said he'd introduce me around to some people who could help my career. Kenny joked that he'd be my agent."

Schrader obviously remembered Irvan's slow times, too.

"As I came back around after getting the Daytona 500 checkered flag I was enjoying this absolute euphoria," said Irvan. "All of a sudden I felt this big crunch on my car from behind. It was Schrader. He'd bumped me, then he pulled alongside with the biggest grin I ever saw."

If Irvan had looked in the mirror right then it's likely he'd have seen an even bigger grin—his own.

Irvan accepts some friendly advice from Rusty Wallace, the 1989 Winston Cup champion.

LeRoy Neiman
Sketches

Richard Petty

No stranger to NASCAR racing (his early Daytona 500 poster is a much sought after collector piece), artist LeRoy Neiman sketches Richard Petty in a style that befits "The King".

DAYTONA 500 MILE RACE

SUNDAY FEB. 25

PRODUCED BY **TelePrompTer**

CLOSED CIRCUIT TELEVISION

PIT PARADE

Pit row at Daytona International Speedway prior to the running of the Daytona 500 by STP is a magnet for the mighty of the sport. Some eminent examples follow.

Chairmen of the Board. International Speedway Corp.'s Bill France Jr. and Penske Corp.'s Roger Penske

A three term U.S. Senator from Tennessee, Jim Sasser handled his duties as Grand Marshall of the Daytona 500 with aplomb, as might be expected of the Chairman of the powerful Senate Budget Committee. He's shown in a pre-race huddle with Darrell Waltrip, the 1989 winner. Sasser's good wishes weren't enough to overcome a late race accident just as Waltrip was poised to make his charge for the checker with fuel to spare and no pit stop in his plans.

1990 Daytona 500 winner Derrike Cope

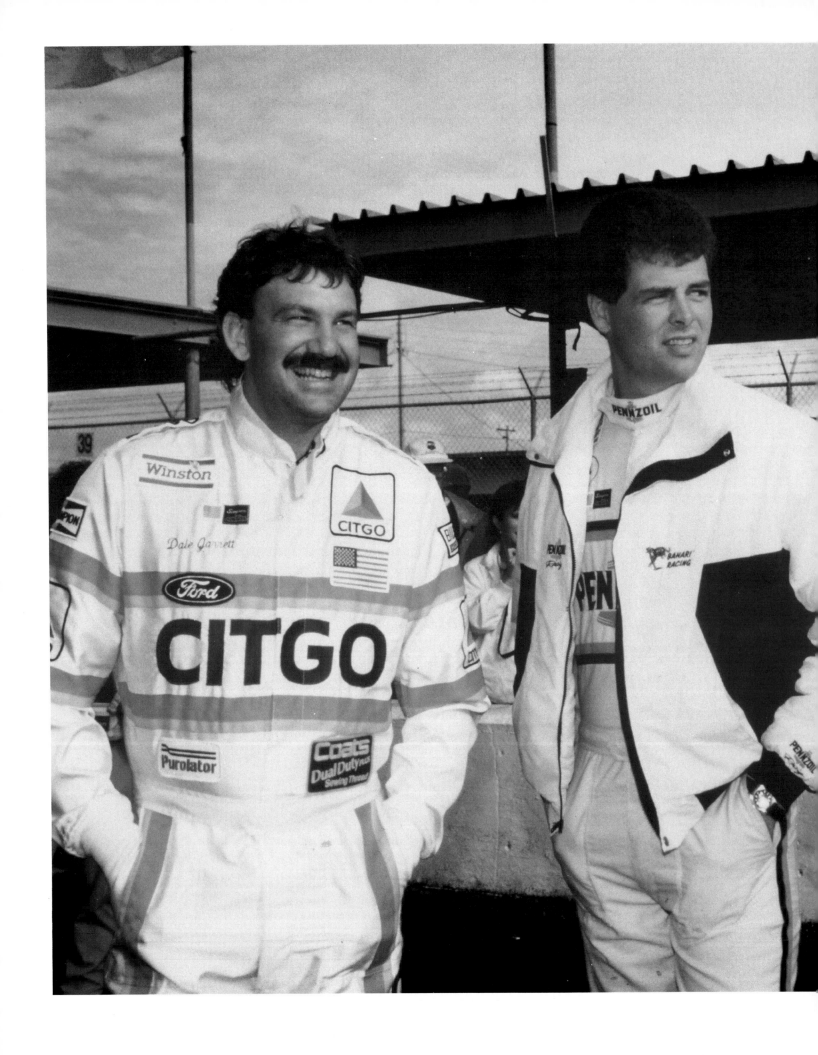

Drivers Dale Jarrett, Michael Waltrip, and Dorsey Schroeder

Driver Ricky Rudd, wife Linda

Car owner Junior Johnson

Car owner Kenny Bernstein, crew chief Larry McReynolds

Crew chief Dale Inman of Richard Petty's STP backed team

Car owner Robert Yates

Driver Alan Kulwicki

Driver Bill Elliott, Talladega Superspeedway President Mike Helton

Car owner Felix Sabates, driver Darrell Waltrip

Team manager Steve Hmeil, crew chief Robin Pemberton, and driver Mark Martin

Drivers Geoff and Brett Bodine, following NASCAR's family tradition

Car owner Jack Roush

Crew chief Jeff Hammond, driver Darrell Waltrip

Buddy Baker, back as a driver, Chuck Rider

Car owner Rick Hendrick

Car owner Leonard Wood

Television's Jay Leno

The last shall be first. Relegated to a last place starting position for the second segment of the Busch Clash by virtue of winning the first segment, Dale Earnhardt wasted no time getting back in front.

BUSCH CLASH

DALE'S DASH
FROM LAST PLACE TO FIRST

By Tom Higgins

Dale Earnhardt made what even he termed an "unbelievable charge", dashing quickly from 14th (and last) in the Busch Clash's second segment to win the special event race for the fourth time in six tries.

Driving his Chevrolet on the track's inside edge, Earnhardt surprised even himself by passing 13 rivals in just 1½ laps around the 2.5 mile trioval layout. He was barely challenged for the rest of the final 10 lap segment of the new format race, which annually matches the previous season's NASCAR Winston Cup Series pole winners and a wild card entry. Earnhardt started the last 25 mile portion from the rear of the pack because he also won the first half, after which the field was inverted for the first time in the event's history for the 25 mile "finale". After a caution period "halftime", Earnhardt whipped from 14th to 9th on lap 11. Hugging the apron, he surged all the way ahead going down the speedway's long backstretch. Earnhardt then, rather easily, held off Mark Martin, whose Ford finished two car lengths back, and Rusty Wallace, who was

third in a Pontiac.

Trailing in order: Bill Elliott, Ford; Kyle Petty, Pontiac; Geoff Bodine, Ford; Ernie Irvan, Chevy; Alan Kulwicki, Ford; Brett Bodine, Buick; Greg Sacks, Chevy; Dick Trickle, Pontiac; Ken Schrader, Chevy; Ricky Rudd, Chevy; and Derrike Cope, Chevy.

An accident in turn 4 on lap 12 eliminated the latter three drivers, who were unhurt.

"My car worked well off the bottom of the track, no matter what kind of air (aerodynamic slipstream) was around it," said Earnhardt. "The wind, the drafting condition, was so good down there I decided to hold that line and when I came off turn two I knew I was going to the front."

Earnhardt started the first segment in sixth position and took the lead on lap 2, which meant he wound up being the frontrunner for 18 of the 20 laps.

He was followed to the line in the first segment by Irvan, Schrader, and Rudd. That segment paid 40% of the $280,000 purse.

"Man, that car really came around the track," Earnhardt said of the second segment sprint.

"It was awesome, wasn't it? All week long we (the Richard Childress Racing team, led by crew chief Kirk Shelmerdine) thought about strategy. We even thought about not winning the first half so we wouldn't have to start at the rear. But we decided we're a 'go for it' team and settled on trying to get it all. I can't believe we came from the back to the front in two laps. I told everyone earlier in the week that King Kong couldn't do that."

Earnhardt averaged 189.474 mph and took home a well earned $60,000.

"It's disappointing to see Dale come back and dominate," said Mark Martin, remembering that Earnhardt overwhelmed the opposition at Daytona in 1990 only to have a cut tire cost him the Daytona 500 in the last mile. "We should have seen this coming. He was playing games with everyone in practice the past two days."

Said one NASCAR insider, "Dale just drove a stake through the heart of every team in the garage area."

Dale Earnhardt accomplished the near impossible feat of coming from the last starting position to the top finishing position in only 2 laps in the second segment of the Busch Clash. Having taken the first segment he deservedly pocketed the $60,000 lion's share of the spoils for the rich race open to the fastest Winston Cup drivers.

Geoff Bodine's Budweiser Ford got no special treatment in the Busch Clash, sponsored by another Anheuser-Busch brand. He ended up out of the drafting line for a tenth place finish in the first segment.

1991 BUSCH CLASH—FIRST 10 LAP SEGMENT
February 10, 1991
OFFICIAL RESULTS

FIN POS	STR POS	CAR NO.	DRIVER	TEAM/CAR	LAPS	MONEY	STATUS
1	6	3	DALE EARNHARDT	GM Goodwrench Chevrolet	10	$25,000	Running
2	9	4	ERNIE IRVAN	Kodak Film Chevrolet	10	17,500	Running
3	11	25	KEN SCHRADER	Kodiak Chevrolet	10	12,500	Running
4	13	9	BILL ELLIOTT	Coors Light Ford	10	9,000	Running
5	14	5	RICKY RUDD	Tide Chevrolet	10	7,000	Running
6	12	6	MARK MARTIN	Folgers Coffee Ford	10	6,000	Running
7	2	42	KYLE PETTY	Mello Yello Pontiac	10	5,500	Running
8	5	26	BRET BODINE	Quaker State Buick	10	5,000	Running
9	1	10	DERRIKE COPE	Purolator Chevrolet	10	4,500	Running
10	3	7	ALAN KULWICKI	U.S. Army Ford	10	4,000	Running
11	10	2	RUSTY WALLACE	Miller Genuine Draft Pontiac	10	4,000	Running
12	7	66	DICK TRICKLE	TropArtic Pontiac	10	4,000	Running
13	8	18	GREG SACKS	U.S. Navy Chevrolet	10	4,000	Running
14	4	11	GEOFF BODINE	Budweiser Ford	10	4,000	Running

1991 BUSCH CLASH—SECOND 10 LAP SEGMENT
February 10, 1991
OFFICIAL RESULTS

FIN POS	STR POS	CAR NO.	DRIVER	TEAM/CAR	LAPS	MONEY	STATUS
1	14	3	DALE EARNHARDT	GM Goodwrench Chevrolet	10	$35,000	Running
2	9	6	MARK MARTIN	Folgers Coffee Ford	10	25,000	Running
3	4	2	RUSTY WALLACE	Miller Genuine Draft Pontiac	10	20,000	Running
4	11	9	BILL ELLIOTT	Coors Light Ford	10	17,000	Running
5	8	42	KYLE PETTY	Mello Yello Pontiac	10	12,000	Running
6	1	11	GEOFF BODINE	Budweiser Ford	10	8,000	Running
7	13	4	ERNIE IRVAN	Kodak Film Chevrolet	10	7,500	Running
8	5	7	ALAN KULWICKI	U.S. Army Ford	10	7,000	Running
9	7	26	BRETT BODINE	Quaker State Buick	10	6,500	Running
10	2	18	GREG SACKS	U.S. Navy Chevrolet	10	6,000	Running
11	3	66	DICK TRICKLE	TropArtic Pontiac	10	6,000	Running
12	12	25	KEN SCHRADER	Kodiak Chevrolet	2	6,000	Accident
13	10	5	RICKY RUDD	Tide Chevrolet	2	6,000	Accident
14	6	10	DERRIKE COPE	Purolator Chevrolet	1	6,000	Accident

TIME OF RACE: 00:15:50
AVERAGE SPEED: 189.474 mph

MARGIN OF VICTORY: 2 car lengths
LEAD CHANGES: 4 lead changes, 2 drivers

TRUE VALUE DODGE INTERNATIONAL RACE OF CHAMPIONS

SCOTT PRUETT'S COMEBACK TRAIL LEADS TO VICTORY CIRCLE

Scott Pruett outran an all-star field of NASCAR, CART Indy Car, IMSA and SCCA drivers, all mounted on equally prepared Dodge Daytonas, to win the opening True Value Dodge International Race of Champions at Daytona International Speedway. Two weekends earlier Pruett had proved that he was fit and fast, recovered from the Indy Car testing accident injuries that kept him on the sidelines for the entire 1990 season. He did this by taking his Bud Light Jaguar into the lead of the SunBank 24 at Daytona for the Rolex Cup within the first hour. All chance for the Rolex Cup evaporated with mechanical failure before dawn. Nonetheless, the gritty driver of the Budweiser-backed Truesports Indy Car entry made his point in the 24 Hours; he was back and capable of winning. His year long devotion to a strenuous physical therapy regime was beginning to pay dividends.

Payoff it did in the IROC contest, 26 points and the lead for grabbing the lion's share of the $670,000 purse split among the 12 drivers in the four race series at season's end.

NASCAR luminary Bill Elliott led twice for a total of four laps but had to concede the last six and the winner's trophy to Pruett.

Pre-race favorite NASCAR champion Dale Earnhardt, also the 1990 IROC Champion, led the first four laps from his number two starting position (all starting positions were drawn by lot) but became the victim of an early race tapping incident involving eventual runner-up Elliott. Another comeback trail driver, Al Unser, a four time Indianapolis 500 winner, placed third, indicating that the leg he broke last season in an Indy Car accident had fully mended. He started all the way back in 11th place, on the last row alongside Rusty Wallace. Wallace hustled to the front early, took over from Earnhardt for the lead on lap 5, led on two other occasions, faded to 10th at the end. IMSA driver Bob Wollek, fresh from a victory in the Daytona 24 Hours, his fourth, found the full 2.5 mile trioval a bit of a learning experience, crashed on his own after 37 of the 40 laps. Al Unser, Jr., a former IROC champion and the current CART Indy Car champion, followed his father home in fourth place. IROC newcomer Tommy Kendall, the SCCA Trans-Am champion, acquitted himself well with a 5th place finish, followed by NASCAR's Geoff Bodine and Mark Martin. IMSA's Geoff Brabham, starting on the pole, and Dorsey Schroeder placed 8th and 9th.

Elliott felt he had a good shot at a swift and smiling Pruett until he collected some debris from Wollek's car on the last lap and came close to collecting the wall as well.

TRUE VALUE DODGE INTERNATIONAL RACE OF CHAMPIONS (IROC XV)
February 15, 1991
OFFICIAL RESULTS

FIN POS	STR POS	CAR NO.	DRIVER/DODGE COLOR	LAPS	POINTS	STATUS
1	5	5	SCOTT PRUETT/Black	40	26	Running
2	7	7	BILL ELLIOTT/Red	40	17	Running
3	11	11	AL UNSER/Bright Blue	40	14	Running
4	6	6	AL UNSER, JR./Mustard	40	14	Running
5	3	3	TOMMY KENDALL/Aqua	40	10	Running
6	9	9	GEOFF BODINE/Yellow	40	9	Running
7	10	10	MARK MARTIN/Rose	40	8	Running
8	1	1	GEOFF BRABHAM/Dark Blue	40	7	Running
9	8	8	DORSEY SCHROEDER/Pink	40	6	Running
10	12	12	RUSTY WALLACE/Lime	40	8	Running
11	4	4	BOB WOLLEK/Tan	37	4	Accident
12	2	2	DALE EARNHARDT/Orange	12	3	Accident

TIME OF RACE: 00:32:31
AVERAGE SPEED: 184.521 mph
MARGIN OF VICTORY: 1 car length

LEAD CHANGES: 13 lead changes, 6 drivers
PRIZE MONEY: The total IROC purse of $670,000 will be paid upon conclusion of the series, based on points.

Twelve of Motorsports' Brightest Stars…The starting cast in the True Value Dodge International Race of Champions featured headliners Dale Earnhardt, Tom Kendall, Scott Pruett, Geoff Bodine, Al Unser Jr. and dad Al Unser, Mark Martin, Bob Wollek, Bill Elliott, Dorsey Schroeder, Geoff Brabham, and Rusty Wallace.

GOODY'S 300 FOR BUSCH GRAND NATIONAL CARS

A REPEAT VICTORY FOR DALE EARNHARDT, CRASHES AGAIN ABOUND

The '91 Goody's 300 had a lot in common with the '90 Goody's 300. Dale Earnhardt and his GM Goodwrench Chevrolet prevailed handily and accidents eliminated a sizeable portion of the field early. This year's major pile-up involved "only" fifteen cars, as opposed to twenty-three in 90's premier tangle, and happened on the first lap, well behind a flying Earnhardt. By the 100 mile mark, almost one third of the 43 car starting field had been eliminated by this incident and two others to follow. Todd Bodine required five stitches as the most seriously injured crash victim.

If anything, Earnhardt had an easier victory this time around, since he wasn't required to make up a lap due to an oil leak induced black flag as in '90. Once the yellow caution flag was furled after lap 11, Earnhardt quickly disposed of the front row qualifi-

ers, Busch Grand National tour regulars David Green and Jack Sprague. He led 90 of the 120 laps, including the last 20. The final stages of the race amounted to a 4 car train, consisting of Earnhardt, Davey Allison, Michael Waltrip, and Ken Schrader. Despite valiant attempts, none of the latter trio could make any real run at Earnhardt. Waltrip's Pennzoil Pontiac did displace Allison's Havoline Chevrolet for second place. Runner-up Waltrip gave the winner full marks, "Today, he was faster." The Winston Cup drivers, as usual, gave the Busch Grand National contingent no sympathy and no place on the victory podium. Harry Gant in the Skoal Bandit Buick was fifth ahead of the best placed Busch regular, Tom Peck in the Thomas Chevrolet Olds. Morgan Shepherd placed seventh in the Texas Pete

Ford, just ahead of Jimmy Spencer. Rookie honors went to 9th place Randy MacDonald. Rising star Kenny Wallace rounded out the top ten.

Once again, Darrell Waltrip was an innocent victim, this time of a tangle initially involving Dale Jarrett and Jimmy Spencer. This one collected Chuck Bown as well, with only Spencer able to continue. As might be expected, the multiple crashes knocked the average speed down—to a modest 144.192 mph, despite some late race laps by the leading quartet in excess of 190 mph.

For his third Goody's 500 win, Earnhardt pocketed $38,352 and posted a perfect 1.000 batting average for all three '91 Speed Weeks events he had entered to date. He'd trade them all for one Daytona 500 victory circle trip.

GOODY'S 300 NASCAR BUSCH GRAND NATIONAL SERIES RACE
February 16, 1991
OFFICIAL RESULTS

FIN POS	STR POS	CAR NO.	DRIVER	TEAM/CAR	LAPS	POINTS	MONEY	STATUS
1	3	3	DALE EARNHARDT	GM Goodwrench Chevrolet	120	180	$38,532	Running
2	18	30	MICHAEL WALTRIP	Pennzoil Pontiac	120	170	25,757	Running
3	7	28	DAVEY ALLISON	Havoline Chevrolet	120	165	18,625	Running
4	4	15	KEN SCHRADER	Exxon Chevrolet	120	160	13,900	Running
5	35	7	HARRY GANT	Skoal Buick	120	155	12,707	Running
6	6	96	TOM PECK	Thomas Racing Oldsmobile	120	150	26,546	Running
7	25	97	MORGAN SHEPHERD	Texas Pete Sauces Ford	120	146	12,007	Running
8	20	45	JIMMY SPENCER	Lowes Foods Pontiac	119	142	8,357	Running
9	8	16	RANDY MACDONALD	IMARC Games Pontiac	119	138	6,900	Running
10	19	36	KENNY WALLACE	Cox Treated Lumber Pontiac	119	134	20,146	Running
11	10	4	BOBBY HILLIN	MCO Plus Chevrolet	119	130	6,657	Running
12	31	52	BUTCH MILLER	31-W Insulation Oldsmobile	118	127	5,500	Running
13	5	56	TOMMY ELLIS	Polaroid Fancamera Buick	118	124	15,546	Running
14	43	9	JOE BESSEY[†]	Holden Agency Oldsmobile	117	121	9,750	Running
15	40	27	ELTON SAWYER	Gwaltney Big 8's Buick	116	118	11,871	Running
16	14	6	TOMMY HOUSTON	Rose's Stores Buick	114	115	12,346	Running
17	12	79	DAVE REZENDES	Champion TV Rental Oldsmobile	114	112	9,696	Running
18	41	08	BOBBY DOTTER	Team R. Racing Buick	114	109	8,439	Running
19	39	00	L. D. OTTINGER	Beard Oil Oldsmobile	113	106	8,896	Running
20	21	59	ROBERT PRESSLEY	Alliance Training Oldsmobile	110	103	8,546	Engine
21	16	87	JOE NEMECHEK	Mothers Polishers Chevrolet	110	100	7,189	Running
22	29	05	RICHARD LASATER*	Eclipse Racing Pontiac	103	97	4,200	Running
23	23	5	ED BERRIER	Garner's Preserves Oldsmobile	90	94	4,614	Running
24	33	99	JEFF BURTON	Armour Meats Chevrolet	73	91	9,246	Running
25	30	31	STEVE GRISSOM	Grissom Racing Oldsmobile	44	88	8,896	Running
26	28	38	BRAD TEAGUE	Teague & Weiss Oldsmobile	37	85	3,500	Handling
27	32	34	TODD BODINE	C&W Racing Buick	30	82	4,307	Accident
28	2	48	JACK SPRAGUE	StaffAmerica Oldsmobile	29	79	5,239	Accident
29	13	11	JACK INGRAM	Skoal Chevrolet	28	76	4,914	Engine
30	1	8	DAVID GREEN*	TIC Financial Systems Oldsmobile	23	73	3,850	Accident
31	9	32	DALE JARRETT	Nestle Crunch Pontiac	16	70	4,957	Accident
32	22	17	DARRELL WALTRIP	Western Auto Chevrolet	16	67	3,150	Accident
33	17	63	CHUCK BOWN	Nescafe Classic Pontiac	16	64	6,946	Accident
34	24	57	TIM BENDER	Orchard Park RediMix Chevrolet	14	61	3,050	Accident
35	37	72	TRACY LESLIE*	Detroit Gasket Oldsmobile	1	58	4,650	Accident
36	11	94	BOBBY LABONTE	Penrose Firecracker Oldsmobile	0	55	4,596	Accident
37	15	51	MIKE MCLAUGHLIN*	Wheels Discount Auto Oldsmobile	0	52	3,825	Accident
38	26	81	DAVEY JOHNSON	Daily's Juices Pontiac	0	49	3,589	Accident
39	27	25	JIMMY HENSLEY	Beverly Racing Oldsmobile	0	46	6,146	Accident
40	34	14	JOE THURMAN	Thurman Enterprises Oldsmobile	0	43	2,700	Accident
41	36	10	ERNIE IRVAN	MAC Tools Chevrolet	0	40	3,557	Accident
42	38	92	DICK TRICKLE	Custom Veneers Chevrolet	0	37	2,700	Accident
43	42	12	KEN BOUCHARD[†]	ADAP Auto Parts Pontiac	0	34	3,700	Accident

TIME OF RACE: 02:04:50
AVERAGE SPEED: 144.192 mph
MARGIN OF VICTORY: .67 second
*Vortex Comics Rookie of the Year Candidate

CAUTION FLAGS: 4 flags for 35 laps
LEAD CHANGES: 9 lead changes, 6 drivers
[†] Busch Grand National North Driver

FORTUNE AND A YELLOW FLAG FINISH SMILE ON WINNER BEN HESS

Lady Luck awarded the '90 ARCA 200 to Jimmy Horton and, in typically fickle fashion, snatched victory away from him in the '91 contest. This year's beneficiary of the yellow caution flag was Ben Hess, in an Oldsmobile he'd never seen until a week before the race. With the race almost two thirds complete, Horton was leading handily in his Miles Concrete Chevrolet when one of the seven caution flags waved, enabling Hess to cut down on his lead. With only six laps to go there was another caution. This time Horton's fuel pick up failed to operate correctly and he was an easy victim, eventually finishing fourth. A start/finish line tangle behind Hess and second place finisher Bobby Bowsher in

the Don Thompson Excavating Ford brought out the final yellow caution flag, allowing Hess to win without facing any last lap challenge. Oldsmobile mounted Kenny Teague was the third place finisher.

Star performer in the early going was surprise polesitter Dorsey Schroeder, a new recruit from the road racing ranks, who held the lead for the first 15 laps. Schroeder's place in the sun evaporated when he tagged Bowsher's Ford on the first pit stop, rearranging his own car's bodywork in somewhat unaerodynamic fashion. Out of contention, Schroeder soldiered on to a 10th place finish.

Two crowd pleasing ARCA 200 perennials, Charlie Glotzbach

and Red Farmer, had bad days. Glotzbach's third engine of the week lasted only 16 laps, the number of places he had moved up in the field at this early stage. A highly competitive Farmer, third on the starting grid, cut a tire on lap 5, involved Ferrell Harris and Bill Venturini in the resultant spin. Only Farmer was injured.

The low 128.480 mph winning average speed reflects the number and length of the caution periods but detracted not at all from Hess' jubilation. When he hustled his new car into fourth place in qualifying, he knew he had a good shot at victory and needed only a little luck to prevail. He got it.

28TH ANNUAL ARCA PERMATEX SUPERCAR SERIES RACE
February 10, 1991
OFFICIAL RESULTS

FIN POS	STR POS	CAR NO.	DRIVER	TEAM/CAR	LAPS	STATUS
1	4	40	BEN HESS	Salem National Lease Oldsmobile	80	Running
2	7	21	BOBBY BOWSHER	Don Thompson Exc-Bobby Fisher Ford	80	Running
3	6	03	KERRY TEAGUE	Radiator Specialty-NuPower Olds	80	Running
4	2	80	JIM HORTON	S&H Racing-Miles Concrete Chevrolet	80	Running
5	26	87	JOE NIEMIROSKI	Boardwalk Auto Sales Oldsmoble	80	Running
6	38	16	ROY PAYNE	Mopar-Hamner Racing Engines Chrysler	80	Running
7	9	58	SCOTT HANSEN	Air Orlando Chevrolet	80	Running
8	28	47	KEN RAGAN	Ken Kincaid Racing Chevrolet	79	Running
9	13	20	KEITH WAID	Tarrant Hydraulic Service Buick	79	Running
10	1	69	DORSEY SCHROEDER*	NAPA-Valvoline-LC Racing Ford	79	Running
11	34	8	BOB DOTTER	Dotter & Davis Racing Chevrolet	79	Running
12	12	85	BOBBY GERHART	J. Omar Landis-Thomas Chevrolet	79	Running
13	15	33	DALE MCDOWELL	Dover Cylinder Heads Chevrolet	78	Running
14	31	10	GLENN BREWER	Eagle Budweiser-Brown Htg-AC Oldsmobile	78	Running
15	27	04	BOBBY WOODS	Screamin Squeegees Oldsmobile	77	Running
16	5	35	BILL VENTURINI	Amoco Ultimate-Rain X Chevrolet	77	Running
17	32	00	DON WATSON	Dixie Queen Riverboat Chevrolet	77	Running
18	42	76	GRAHAM TAYLOR	Car Mate Trailers Ford	77	Running
19	10	31	CECIL EUNICE	Levin Racing Team Oldsmobile	77	Running
20	29	54	PATTY SIMKO-SCHACHT	Bob Schacht Motorsports Buick	76	Running
21	25	19	CHRIS GEHRKE	Lean Supreme Oldsmobile	76	Running
22	39	88	DAVID BOGGS	Wally Finney Racing Oldsmobile	76	Running
23	19	3	CARL MISKOTTEN JR.	Anglo American Auto Auction Buick	75	Accident
24	14	22	BILLY THOMAS	Thomas Racing Enterprises Pontiac	72	Running
25	18	79	MARK THOMPSON	Gray Racing Chevrolet	71	Accident
26	22	99	DONNIE MORAN	Alpine-Alpa Cheese Chrysler	68	Running
27	23	93	TIM HEPLER	Hepler Racing Chrysler	64	Running
28	36	56	JERRY HILL	Jerry Hill Motorsports Buick	54	Rod
29	17	29	BOB KESELOWSKI	K Automotive Chevrolet	51	Piston
30	35	46	RUSTY JOHNSON	Jody's Place Chevrolet	38	Clutch
31	34	98	MARK GIBSON	Hughes Supply Inc. Oldsmobile	31	Oil Pump
32	41	77	DAVE WELTMEYER	Atlas Copco Tool Buick	29	Transmission
33	33	17	BILLY SIMMONS	S&S Racing Chevrolet	28	Gear Box
34	37	59	JOHN STRADTMAN	Stradtman Motorsports Pontiac	25	Accident
35	11	51	DAVE SIMKO	Mound Steel-Tom Company Oldsmobile	20	Tie Rod
36	40	23	RON BURCHETTE	Pilot Engines Chevrolet	20	Piston
37	30	37	JERRY COOK	Target Expediting Oldsmobile	19	Accident
38	21	28	CHARLIE GLOTZBACH	Floyd Garrett Trucking Chevrolet	16	Push Rod
39	16	26	MIKE DAVIS	Bob Schacht Motorsports Oldsmobile	11	Transmission
40	20	34	BOB BREVAK	Race Glaze Buick	9	Accident
41	8	44	FERREL HARRIS	TT Colley-Ken Allen Pontiac	5	Accident
42	3	74	RED FARMER	NAPA-Valvoline-LC Racing Ford	5	Accident

TIME OF RACE: 01:33:24
AVERAGE SPEED: 128.480 mph
MARGIN OF VICTORY: finished under caution

CAUTION FLAGS: 7 flags for 24 laps
LEAD CHANGES: 10 lead changes, 3 drivers
*Talladega Pole Position Qualifier

Eventual winner Ben Hess in the Salem National Lease Oldsmobile leads a closely knit pack in the early going.

Donnie Moran's Alpina Alpa Cheese Chrysler was one of three entered in the ARCA 200. Best placed was
Roy Payne's Mopar-Hammer entry, the sixth place finisher.

FLORIDA 200 NASCAR DASH

SCOTT HERBERG PICKS DAYTONA'S HIGH BANKS FOR HIS FIRST RACING VICTORY

Young New Jerseyan Scott Herberg "borrowed" his father's Pontiac for a Friday afternoon spin in the Florida sunshine, returned it an hour and a half later wearing the three foot tall Florida 200 victory trophy as a hood ornament. For the 21 year old driver it was a maiden trip to the winner's circle. Herberg qualified his dad's Luck's Country Foods Pontiac fifth, never slipped below sixth in the 200 mile event, as a charter member of the lead pack. He first picked up the lead position on lap 22 on pit stops by the other front runners, later got shuffled back to the fourth spot after polesitter Mike Swaim, Gary Wade Finley, and Robert Huffman, all Pontiac mounted, encountered difficulties, leaving Herberg two laps up on Dale Howdyshell's Ford at the end.

David Probst, another Pontiac driver, took down third place. Despite his lack of a challenge in the closing stages, Herberg can take comfort in always being in contention, playing the fuel stops adroitly, and husbanding his mechanical resources like a professional driver should, a professional driver who's just had his biggest payday—$11,850.

FLORIDA 200 NASCAR DASH SERIES RACE
February 15, 1991
OFFICIAL RESULTS

FIN POS	STR POS	CAR NO.	DRIVER	TEAM/CAR	LAPS	MONEY	STATUS
1	5	09	SCOTT HERBERG	Lucks Country Style Foods Pontiac	80	$11,850	Running
2	7	71	DALE HOWDYSHELL	Howdyshell Racing Ford	78	7,500	Running
3	22	88	DAVID PROBST	Congoleum Vinyl Flooring Pontiac	78	5,800	Running
4	19	8	ROGER REUSE	Alabama Controls, Inc. Pontiac	77	4,350	Out Of Gas
5	27	57	DAVID HEFFINGER	W.D. Allen Racing Pontiac	77	3,750	Running
6	6	33	STANTON BARRETT	Interstate Batteries Pontiac	77	3,300	Running
7	8	77	JOHNNY CHAPMAN	Douglas & Sons Trucking Pontiac	77	3,050	Running
8	23	28	MERRILL WALKER	Engineering & Mfg. Service Pontiac	77	2,850	Running
9	21	4	GARY WADE FINLEY	Cindy York Racing Pontiac	76	2,650	Engine
10	16	75	ROBERT HUFFMAN	Custom Material Handling Pontiac	75	2,750	Engine
11	2	25	LEE FARTHING	MOPAR-Tom Johnson Camping World Dodge	75	2,200	Engine
12	11	22	MAXIE BUSH	Bush Racing Pontiac	75	2,100	Running
13	1	21	MIKE SWAIM	Watson Automotive Pontiac	75	2,300	Engine
14	9	52	DEAN COMBS	Quaker State-Tom Johnson Camping Chevrolet	74	1,900	Engine
15	35	45	BILL HENNECY	Hickman Brothers Trucking Pontiac	61	1,825	Engine
16	37	04	THAD COLEMAN	Furr Construction Chevrolet	61	1,725	Rear End
17	18	29	CHARLES STALEY	Cobra Electronics-Tony Lama Pontiac	57	1,700	Engine
18	15	07	GEORGE CRENSHAW	Crenshaw Racing Pontiac	57	1,650	Running
19	31	51	JOHNNY BALDWIN	Baldwin Auto Parts Pontiac	54	1,600	Running
20	10	11	DARRELL MARSHALL	Marshall Const-Staunton Building Pontiac	48	1,550	Fire
21	33	20	JEFF MONTGOMERY	Diesel Electronics-Nichels Eng. Pontiac	48	1,525	Running
22	13	24	MICKEY YORK	Cobra Electronics Pontiac	46	1,500	Engine
23	32	34	MILTON BRECHEEN	Diamond Racing Engines-Pell Auto Pontiac	46	1,425	Running
24	30	17	FRED PARISIAN	A&T Engines Pontiac	42	1,400	Engine
25	36	90	JOHN NANCE	King Of The Hill Racing Ent. Ford	29	1,350	Running
26	25	98	R. D. HAMPTON	Creative Critters Pontiac	24	1,300	Trans.
27	20	2	SCOTT WEAVER	C&S Machine Shop-Carolina Paint Chevrolet	23	1,275	Engine
28	41	54	JOE BOOHER	Booher Farms-Down The Hatch Pontiac	20	1,250	Bearing
29	14	02	FLEET CREWS	Crews Tool & Equip-Glover Engines Pontiac	19	1,175	Overheat
30	4	48	MICHAEL LEATHERS	Irmo Racing-Racing Radio's Nissan	19	1,150	Engine
31	26	35	DON GUIGNARD	Buy American Products Pontiac	16	1,120	Engine
32	24	67	CLAUDE GWIN JR.	Autry Ent-Hy-Glass Body Shop Pontiac	16	1,100	Oil Press.
33	28	03	JIM KERLEY	Exclusive Body Works Pontiac	14	1,075	Oil Pump
34	38	99	GARY MOORE	Moore Racing Chevrolet	12	1,025	Trans.
35	34	95	RODNEY ORR	Beacher Orr Contractor Pontiac	11	975	Engine
36	40	42	ED HOLEWIAK JR.	Texaco & Mutual Oil Pontiac	10	970	Trans.
37	17	78	CHRIS BROWN	Brake Tech Pontiac	4	960	Engine
38	3	16	DUELL STURGILL	Mercruiser-Mantra Boats Ford	4	950	Engine
39	12	00	KEVIN BROOKSHIRE	WSSL Radio Pontiac	4	925	Engine
40	39	5	DAN HARDY	Jagermeister & Nissan Datsun	3	900	Oil Leak
41	29	13	MICHAEL ANGLIN	Carrollwood Letter Carriers Pontiac	0	900	Engine

TIME OF RACE: 1:29:41
AVERAGE SPEED: 133.804 mph
MARGIN OF VICTORY: 2 laps

CAUTION FLAGS: 4 flags for 13 laps
LEAD CHANGES: 12 lead changes, 5 drivers

Start of the Florida 200. Front row occupants Mike Swaim in the Watson Automotive Pontiac and Lee Farthing in the Mopar-Tom Johnson Dodge both succumbed to engine problems. Young Scott Herberg in his father's Luck's Country Style Foods Pontiac prevailed from a third row starting position.

Will the real Kyle Petty stand up? Lifelike Petty cutout enables fans of Petty and his Mello Yello Pontiac team to be photographed with their hero even when he's not around.